Awakening Hanuman Within

AWAKENING HANUMAN WITHIN

A Journey to Strength, Devotion and Fearlessness

Shashika Mooruth

URJA
MUSIC

For more information about the author, please visit
www.shashikamooruth.com

First published in 2025 by Urja Music

P-ISBN: 978-93-342-7550-6

URJA MUSIC (PTY) LTD
www.urjamusic.com

For enquiries: urjamusic@urjamusic.com

Printed and bound in India

To my parents,
who nurtured me to live a life
rooted in culture and guided by spirituality.

ॐ अज्ञानतिमिरान्धस्य ज्ञानाञ्जनशलाकया ।
चक्षुरुन्मीलितं येन तस्मै श्रीगुरवे नमः ॥

om ajñāna-timirāndhasya jñānāñjana-śalākayā
chakṣur unmīlitaṁ yena tasmai śrī-gurave namaḥ

I was born in the darkest ignorance, and my spiritual master opened my eyes with the torch of knowledge. I offer my respectful obeisances unto him

~ Guru Gita

Contents

A Note Before We Begin

For the sake of narrative flow, Hanumanji is referred to simply as "Hanuman" throughout most of this book. However, it is with the utmost reverence that He is traditionally addressed as "Hanumanji" or "Shri Hanuman." The suffix 'ji' is a mark of respect and endearment, while 'Shri' signifies auspiciousness and divine presence.

This choice has been made solely to support readability and storytelling clarity, and in no way diminishes the devotion and honour intended toward Lord Hanuman. The same approach applies to Rama, Sita, and all other revered personalities mentioned in this book.

1

The Journey Begins

O Shri Hanumanji,
grant me strength, devotion and wisdom.
May I walk in Your footsteps,
fear nothing, and serve with love.
Let Your energy flow through me,
guiding my every action.

~ Shashika Mooruth

I was raised in South Africa in a home filled with culture and spiritual traditions that shaped my path and purpose. My parents lovingly guided me to learn shlokas, those sacred verses offered in praise of the Divine, with a special focus on the Shri Hanuman Chalisa. Over the years, constant recitation helped me commit the verses to memory, but as I grew older, I realised that reciting them without reflection or a focus on inner transformation was not enough.

I began to reflect on the stories of Hanuman, like lifting a mountain, crossing an ocean, or tearing open His chest to reveal Lord Rama in His heart. While these feats may seem impossible in today's world, they do not diminish the greatness and power that Hanuman embodies. I asked myself how these stories could serve my spiritual growth.

The question stirred a deep inner search, leading me to explore what truly resonated with me in these ancient leelas, the divine tales woven through time. I realised that the key to understanding their deeper meaning lay in focusing intently during my recitation and appealing to Hanumanji for guidance. In doing so, I discovered that many of my own life experiences mirror these stories, if only we learn to see with the inner eye.

For years, friends had encouraged me to write a book about my spiritual journey and realisations. I would often jot down thoughts or store typed notes away on a hard drive, never quite gathering the resolve to weave them together. Then one day, while visiting my son's home, a profound thought arose, as though Lord Krishna Himself had whispered it to me: "Yes, you should write, but this is the book to write first." The title came effortlessly, Awakening Hanuman Within.

At that moment, I didn't fully understand why this particular book was meant to be written. But as I began to pull out notes I had penned over the years and sift through them, deciding what would be relevant, I realised how deeply the essence of Hanuman's stories resonates with me. So, I started to organise them.

However, I didn't want the book to be just a collection of mantras and traditional references. I wanted it to offer practical insights, showing how Hanuman's strength, courage, and devotion could apply to our fast-paced world. After all, we aren't tasked with flying across oceans or lifting mountains ourselves.

Seeking clarity, I turned to Lord Krishna in prayer, contemplating and asking for guidance. Eventually, I curled up on my carpet and drifted into a semi-sleep state. Suddenly, I awoke with a jolt, feeling as though I had been stirred by a force. A vivid memory flashed through my mind, as though He was urging me to remember. The realisation buzzed within me, a clear reminder of a real-life experience from 2005 when I too, had crossed an ocean without an air ticket. In that moment, I understood, that it was a modern demonstration of Hanuman's spirit.

In 2005, before the era of e-tickets, my Guruji invited me to Iran for a kirtan performance, where I was to chant devotional hymns, offering a spiritual connection through music and prayer. The plan was to fly from Mumbai to Dubai and then to Kish Island in Iran. A contact in Dubai was responsible for arranging my ticket and visa. However, just a few days before departure, he informed me that the arrangements would not be possible. The courier would not reach me in time with the paper tickets, and the visa process would be delayed as a result.

I felt disappointed, knowing how much my absence would let my Guruji down. Yet within me stirred a strong determination. I told the person in Dubai that I would still go to the airport with my luggage. He called it impossible, but I went anyway.

At the Emirates counter, the staff refused to accept my explanation. Even as I pleaded, they insisted that without a ticket, they could not issue a boarding pass which meant I could not pass immigration. Then, in an unexpected turn of events, the chief immigration officer himself happened to be standing nearby. The Emirates staff, clearly irritated, took me to the chief immigration officer hoping that he would explain to me that I could not travel. But without hesitation, the officer surprised everyone by saying, "I have no problem with her travelling." It felt nothing short of miraculous.

The staff still resisted, arguing that my luggage wouldn't make it in time. But just then, the manager of Emirates approached the counter, wondering what the commotion was about, as all counters had closed and I was the last passenger in sight. He listened, reprimanded his staff, and ordered them to put me on the flight with my luggage. He even called Dubai to ensure that my contact would meet me there with the necessary documents. I boarded the plane, much to the disbelief of many.

My resolve to fulfil my Guruji's wish had invoked a divine response. It wasn't physical strength that carried me through, but the unwavering will to serve. In a sense, I too had leapt across an ocean, driven by complete faith.

The joy of this realisation became a powerful inspiration to begin writing this book. Once I committed, I began to feel Hanumanji's presence in subtle yet powerful ways.

One day, after pausing my writing for a break, I decided to go for my daily walk. I usually passed by children playing. But on this particular day, something was different. As I strolled past a parked car, the sacred verses of the Hanuman Chalisa flowed from its speakers. It was a rare and affirming sign, reminding me that I was on the right path.

Then came an even more mystical experience. As I typed my thoughts for the book on my laptop, I suddenly noticed that the words appeared not in Roman script, but in Devanagari, the script used for Sanskrit and Hindi. My laptop had no Devanagari fonts installed. Bewildered, I restarted the device, yet the phenomenon persisted. On checking the language settings, I discovered that Sanskrit had mysteriously been added. Even after attempting to revert to Roman script, the words continued in Devanagari until I eventually deleted the script from the system.
Reflecting on this, I understood it as a divine reminder. In ancient times, communication flowed through Sanskrit, the language of the gods. I felt Hanumanji was affirming His presence, gently reminding me that I was merely an instrument, that this book was not being written by me, but through me.

Just prior to starting the book, I was unwell, but as I wrote, my energy knew no bounds. The world around me faded as my absorption in the writing grew more intense. Looking back, I realise that in writing, I was healing myself. And in healing myself, I offer you this book perhaps to heal, reflect, or simply journey alongside me.

2

Why Awaken Hanuman Within?

In a world filled with distractions and doubts, the path to inner strength and spiritual clarity often feels distant. Yet within each of us lies an untapped reservoir of courage, devotion, and wisdom, qualities embodied by the great Hanuman.

Hanuman is revered as the embodiment of unwavering devotion, selfless service, immense strength, and deep wisdom. His role in the Ramayana as the greatest devotee of Lord Rama signifies the pinnacle of devotion and surrender.

In our spiritual journey, Hanuman represents the ideal seeker who transcends ego and dedicates every action to the Divine. By meditating on Hanuman, we cultivate the virtues necessary for spiritual elevation namely faith, humility, courage, and surrender. His presence in our journey reassures us that with steadfast devotion and purity of heart, we can overcome any obstacle and reach the ultimate truth.

Yet in the world today, it's easy for worship to sometimes become a routine or a habit, performed without fully reflecting on its deeper significance. Many of us may find ourselves reciting prayers or performing rituals without fully internalising the essence of what they represent. The true beauty of worship is not just in the external acts, but in the heartfelt connection that allows us to awaken the divine qualities of Hanuman within ourselves.

It's not simply about bowing before His deity; it's about letting His strength, courage, and devotion inspire and transform us from within. When we do this, the divine grace of Hanuman truly manifests in our lives, guiding us on our journey toward spiritual growth.

When we invoke Hanuman internally, we integrate His divine strength into our daily lives. Our fears dissolve, as we recognise our infinite strength. We cultivate resilience, finding the courage to face life's challenges with determination. We embrace service and devotion, discovering the joy of selflessness. We awaken the inner Guru, who guides us with wisdom and discernment.

Living with the awareness of Hanuman's presence within us means approaching our responsibilities, relationships, and aspirations with spiritual strength. In this material world, where challenges and uncertainties often shake our resolve, Hanuman's unwavering faith and dedication serve as a guiding light. Through Him, we learn to act with courage and humility, navigating life's complexities with the clarity of divine wisdom.

By meditating on Hanuman, chanting His name, reciting the Shri Hanuman Chalisa, and embodying His virtues, we move beyond mere rituals and truly integrate His power into our existence. When we understand that Hanuman is not separate from us but a reflection of our highest self, we unlock an unshakeable inner strength that can guide us through every aspect of life.

3

Don't Just Read~Awaken!

This book is not meant for a one-time read. The strength, wisdom, and devotion of Hanumanji already reside within you. They simply await remembrance.

When you return to these pages with an open heart, or reflect on even small sections at a time, you'll begin to notice a quiet transformation within.

This is true of any sacred study. It is not about how much we read, but how deeply we absorb. The more you return with intention, the more the words will reveal their power.

My father once shared a profound observation with me. He noticed that while many devotees regularly attended festivals and temple events, few seemed to embrace inner transformation. He would say, 'They come with devotion, but many still hold on to their old ways and habits.'

His words stayed with me, highlighting the importance of introspection. Visiting a temple is not merely a social activity, it is an opportunity to seek the ultimate truth. Each visit should gift us spiritual insights to reflect on, implement, and grow from before we return for further nourishment. This is how we progress spiritually and make our life on earth meaningful.

In the pursuit of self-realisation, three essential concepts are often emphasised. These practices guide us inward, leading to genuine self-discovery. Without them, we may find ourselves lingering on the surface of devotion, missing the transformative depth it can offer. The three concepts are shravanam, mananam and nididhyasanam.

Shravanam means listening with full attention. In ancient times, it referred to listening to the words of a realised person. Today, this can also include reading scriptures, watching spiritual talks, or listening to discourses. The key is to remain attentive and absorb the wisdom with an open mind.

Mananam means reflecting deeply on what you have heard or read. It involves analysing the knowledge, questioning it, and understanding its deeper meanings. True reflection allows you to internalise the teachings, turning mere words into insights.

Nididhyasanam is the process of meditating on this knowledge and applying them in your daily life. Only through such contemplation can true transformation occur.

In summary:

- Shravanam → listen to the wisdom of the scriptures.
- Mananam → reflect and contemplate to gain clarity.
- Nididhyasanam → meditate and apply the teachings to realise the truth within.

When we approach our spiritual practice through these steps, transformation begins from within. These inner shifts naturally reflect in our thoughts, actions, and interactions with others.

This is how I invite you to read this book, not merely as a collection of words, but as a companion on your journey.

Your soul is not seeking more information.
It's waiting for activation.
Read. Reflect. Realise.

4

Divine Aspects of Hanuman

While I have chosen to focus on these specific aspects of Hanuman, these are by no means the only dimensions of His divine nature.

The beauty of Hanuman's character is that the more one studies the Ramayana, engages in devotion, or reflects on His life, the more layers of His greatness unfold. Every sincere seeker may perceive new qualities and lessons, leading to personal realisations that deepen over time.

Moreover, the stories that exemplify these aspects are not confined to a single theme. Each episode in Hanuman's life often reflects a confluence of virtues. What I have outlined is simply a humble attempt to capture a glimpse of His boundless divinity. May this serve as a starting point for further exploration and inspiration.

Wisdom & Discernment

Hanuman embodies profound wisdom and discernment, helping devotees cultivate the ability to make wise decisions and understand the deeper truths of life.

After Rama and Lakshmana reached Kishkindha in search of Sita, they met Hanuman, who immediately recognised Rama's divinity. Hanuman, in His wisdom, understood that Rama and Sugriva could form a powerful alliance. He led them to Sugriva, the exiled Vanara king, who was living in fear of his brother, Vali.

When Rama asked for Sugriva's help in finding Sita, Sugriva was initially hesitant. He doubted whether he had the strength or resources to assist such a powerful prince. More importantly, Sugriva was fearful, he was preoccupied with his own troubles, as Vali had wrongfully banished him from his kingdom. He felt weak and uncertain about forming an alliance with Rama.

Seeing Sugriva's reluctance, Hanuman stepped in as a wise and trusted advisor. He reminded Sugriva of the importance of dharma, the righteous duty of a king. He explained that forming an alliance with Rama was not just a strategic move but a moral responsibility. His words carried profound wisdom. "A true leader does not hesitate to help the righteous." He urged Sugriva to see beyond his personal fears and recognise the greatness of Rama.

Hanuman assured Sugriva that Rama's divine presence would not only help him reclaim his kingdom but also uplift him spiritually. "Trust in Rama, and He will protect you." Hanuman knew that Sugriva feared Vali's immense strength, but He encouraged Sugriva to place his faith in Rama's divine power.

Hanuman's wisdom cleared Sugriva's doubts, and he decided to form an alliance, promising to help find Sita. In return, Rama agreed to help him defeat Vali and reclaim his throne. True to Hanuman's words, Rama later slayed Vali, reinstating Sugriva as the king of Kishkindha. With his kingdom restored, Sugriva fulfilled his promise by gathering his Vanara army to assist Rama in the search for Sita, leading to the eventual battle against Ravana.

During the battle of Lanka, Ravana's son Meghnath, also known as Indrajit, used mystical weapons to bind Hanuman with the brahmastra, an unbreakable divine weapon. Hanuman, however, had the intelligence to recognise that He could break free but chose not to. By remaining bound, He allowed Himself to be taken to Ravana's court, where He assessed the enemy's strength, located Sita, and set Lanka ablaze. This story illustrates strategic intelligence, patience, and awareness. Hanuman teaches us that true wisdom is not just about having knowledge but knowing when to act and when to remain still. Sometimes, surrendering to a situation can bring greater victories than resistance.

Even the Bhagavad-Gita reminds us that aligning with the Divine inevitably leads to victory. Fear and doubt diminish our strength, while faith and commitment to dharma empower us.

Navigate life's challenges with wisdom, cultivate mindfulness and self-awareness. Before making decisions, pause and reflect. Study the scriptures, contemplate their teachings, and allow their timeless wisdom to guide your actions. In doing so, you will find the clarity and courage to walk your path with confidence and purpose.

Hanuman is known to grant clarity of thought and sharpen the intellect of His devotees. I fondly recall my school days when, before exams, I would chant the buddhi mantra, a sacred invocation to awaken inner wisdom, in seeking His divine guidance. The simple act of invoking Him filled me with confidence and steadiness, reminding me that with His blessings, I could overcome any challenge. That tradition still remains today.

बुद्धिर् बलम् यशो धैर्यम्, निर्भयत्वम् अरोगताम्
अजाड्यम् वाक् पटुत्वम् च, हनुमत् स्मरणात् भवेत् ॥

Buddhir Balam Yasho Dhairyam,
Nirbhayatvam Arogataam
Ajaadyam Vaak Pattutvam Cha,
Hanumat Smaranat Bhavet

By remembering Hanuman, one is blessed with intelligence, strength, fame, courage, fearlessness, good health, alertness, and eloquence in speech.

This mantra is not from the Vedas or Upanishads, but is a popular Sanskrit shloka found in many Hanuman-related texts and traditions. It's often recited by devotees as part of daily Hanuman worship, especially by students and seekers of wisdom.

The following mantras are also not directly from ancient scriptures like the Ramayana or the Mahabharata. However, they are traditional Sanskrit mantras that have been widely used for devotional purposes.

ॐ नमो हनुमते नमः।

Om Namo Hanumate Namah

I bow to Lord Hanuman.

ॐ श्री हनुमते नमः।

Om Shri Hanumate Namah

Salutations to the auspicious Lord Hanuman.

These are considered beej or seed mantras and are powerful due to their vibrational energy. Devotees chant them for strength, courage, and protection.

However, the most well-known prayer invoking wisdom from Hanuman is from the Hanuman Chalisa:

बुद्धिहीन तनु जानिके, सुमिरो पवनकुमार।
बल बुद्धि विद्या देहु मोहि, हरहु कलेश विकार।।

buddhiheen tanu jaanike, sumiro pavan kumar
bal buddhi vidya dehu mohi, harahu kalesh vikaar
Knowing myself to be ignorant, I remember You, Son of the Wind.
Please grant me strength, intelligence, and knowledge, and remove my sorrows and faults.

Two paths ahead.
One power within.
That's the Hanuman in you!

Strength & Fearlessness

Hanuman is the epitome of strength and fearlessness. His immense physical power, along with His courage to face any challenge, serves as an inspiration for those seeking to overcome their own obstacles. His bravery in battle is legendary, showing that no challenge is too great when armed with divine strength.

During the great battle of Lanka, Lakshmana was severely injured by Indrajit's powerful attack. He lay unconscious on the battlefield, and the only way to save him was with the sanjeevani booti, a divine herb that could revive the nearly dead. This herb was found on Dronagiri Mountain in the Himalayas.

When the situation became dire, Jambavan, the wise elder of the Vanaras, suggested that Hanuman retrieve the sanjeevani herb. Without hesitation, Hanuman expanded His form and took a mighty leap from Lanka towards the Himalayas, crossing thousands of miles in a matter of moments.

Upon reaching Dronagiri Mountain, Hanuman faced a challenge, there were many medicinal herbs on the mountain, and He could not identify the sanjeevani booti. Not wanting to waste any time, Hanuman made a quick decision. Instead of searching for the specific herb, He lifted the entire mountain on His shoulders. With incredible speed and strength, He flew back to Lanka, carrying the massive peak effortlessly.

As soon as Hanuman arrived, the divine healers identified the sanjeevani booti and used it to revive Lakshmana. He regained consciousness, and the battle continued. Thanks to Hanuman's intelligence, speed, and selfless devotion, Rama's army was saved from disaster.

Hanuman was faced with uncertainty, but His quick thinking led to an effective solution. He acted out of pure love for Rama and Lakshmana, showing again that devotion empowers us to achieve the impossible. Instead of panicking when He couldn't recognise the herb, He made a bold decision to carry the entire mountain. This reflects His courage to act decisively even in uncertainty.

The moment Jambavan suggested that Hanuman fetch the herb, He did not waste a second in doubt or fear. He immediately took flight, showing His unwavering confidence. His boundless energy and willpower remind us that nothing is beyond our reach if we act with sincerity and faith. His journey involved crossing dangerous landscapes and enemy regions, yet Hanuman remained undaunted. Supernatural beings tried to obstruct His mission. However, He fearlessly fought them off and stayed focused on His goal.

Where does this fearlessness come from? From complete surrender to Lord Rama. He has no ego, no doubt, and no sense of limitation. He teaches us that true strength is not just physical but also mental. Inner and outer strength are needed to overcome obstacles. True power is not about aggression, but about self-control and courage.

Fear flees where Hanuman stands!
Summon His strength,
And no mountain is too great.

Suppose you are faced with a 'mountain' of problems. In today's world, many people find themselves overwhelmed by challenges—issues at home, at work, in relationships, and more. These problems pile up, one after another, forming a massive burden. Sadly, many individuals feel crushed under the weight of their difficulties, and the rising suicide rates are a heartbreaking reflection of this.

But when I think of Hanuman lifting the entire mountain, I see a powerful lesson.

Just as Hanuman carried that immense weight with unwavering strength, we too can learn to carry our own 'mountains' of problems. Face them with courage and resolve. Tackle each issue, one by one, without allowing despair to consume you. Draw strength from Hanuman, knowing that resilience and determination can guide you through even the most daunting challenges. Face one fear each day, no matter how big or small. Chant Hanuman's name whenever you feel weak or afraid. Chant to cultivate mental and physical power.

Another remarkable example of Hanuman's strength and fearlessness is when He confronted and defeated Ravana's son, Akshay Kumar. When Hanuman entered Lanka in search of Sita, He deliberately allowed Himself to be captured by Ravana's soldiers so that He could meet Ravana face to face and warn Him of Lord Rama's power. Ravana, enraged by Hanuman's words, ordered his son Akshay Kumar to capture Hanuman.

Akshay Kumar, a mighty warrior, attacked Hanuman with his army. However, Hanuman fearlessly faced him in battle. With His immense strength, Hanuman effortlessly defeated Akshay Kumar, destroying his chariot and weapons. Despite being outnumbered, Hanuman's courage and devotion gave Him the upper hand.

This showcases Hanuman's bravery, His unwavering confidence, and His righteous spirit. He didn't fight for personal glory but to fulfil His duty towards Lord Rama and Sita. It stands as a testament to how fearlessness, when rooted in a noble cause, can lead to victory against even the most powerful adversaries.

Devotion & Selfless Service

Hanuman's devotion to Lord Rama is unparalleled. His selfless service without any expectation of reward is a testament to the purity of devotion. Through Hanuman, we learn that true devotion is about surrendering oneself to the Divine with love and faith, beyond worldly desires.

One day, after the victory in Lanka and Rama's return to Ayodhya, the courtiers and devotees of Lord Rama gathered in the royal court. Among them were sages, warriors, and Hanuman Himself.

During their discussion, someone praised Hanuman's immense strength and bravery in service to Lord Rama. Another added that His love for Rama was even greater than His power. Curious and playfully skeptical, some courtiers said, "You always claim Rama and Sita reside in Your heart. Can You prove it?"

Without hesitation, Hanuman smiled with unwavering faith. With His mighty hands, He tore open His chest. To the amazement of all, there within His heart shone Lord Rama and Sita in divine radiance. His body had become a temple, His devotion no mere declaration, but His very existence.

While this act is not to be taken literally or imitated, its symbolism is profound. Hanuman did not harm Himself out of recklessness but revealed the truth that lived within Him: a heart completely surrendered to divine love. It reminds us that true devotion is not about outward rituals alone but about internal transformation.

O Hanuman, embodiment of fearless devotion,
You teach us to open our hearts with courage,
To live from truth, not fear,
And to serve with love as our strength.

In our modern times, it's easy to slip into habitual worship, reciting prayers or performing rituals without truly connecting with their essence. We may bow before the deity, yet hold back from opening our hearts. Hanuman teaches us that devotion must be alive, courageous, and transparent. His act becomes a metaphor for authenticity: living from the heart with sincerity, even when it requires vulnerability.

The image of Hanuman, His chest torn open revealing Rama and Sita, is a familiar one from religious calendars in my South African childhood. I admired it then, but only now do I grasp its depth. It speaks to living with fearless integrity, letting our inner truth guide our actions.

As an artist, I'm naturally emotional and sensitive. In earlier years, I would quietly carry my pain. But the commercial world soon taught me that unchecked emotion can be overwhelming. I've learned, often painfully, to strike a balance. While my feelings are the wellspring of my creativity, I've had to learn how to manage them with awareness otherwise. Hanumanji became my guiding force, teaching me how to remain centred, how to rise above hurt, and how to stay aligned with purpose.

For those who struggle with confidence, who feel overshadowed or silenced, who hesitate to step forward, then this chapter is for you. You may be gentle and humble, yet find that your kindness is mistaken for weakness. Perhaps fear lingers inside you, not loud, but quietly holding you back. You know your potential, but when it's time to rise, you freeze.

This is not uncommon. But awareness is the beginning of transformation. Hanumanji shows us that strength isn't just about physical power but it's about having the courage to show up with truth, to act with love, and to live with conviction and confidence.

Suppressing your voice can lead to inner turmoil, anxiety, low self-worth, and emotional blocks. Over time, repressed feelings can harden into anger or resentment. But expressing your truth when guided by love and clarity is not a rebellion. It's a liberation.

Start small. Honour your feelings. Speak when it matters. Let sincerity, conviction, and confidence guide your voice. When you speak from that sacred space within, your words like Hanuman's actions, become an offering. They reflect the Divine within you.

Humility & Righteousness

Hanuman's life is a living example of humility and righteousness. Despite His great powers, He remains humble and always acts with integrity. His actions demonstrate the importance of ethical conduct, fairness, and compassion, teaching us that true strength lies in living according to dharma.

Despite the awe-inspiring feat of carrying the entire Dronagiri mountain of herbs back, Hanuman did not feel superior. He considered it His duty and felt grateful for being entrusted with such a responsibility. Upon returning, He sought no praise but simply handed over the mountain, acknowledging that Rama's will made the task possible.

After successfully finding Sita and setting Lanka ablaze, He could have celebrated His accomplishment. Instead, when He returned to Rama and narrated the events, He showed no pride. Rather than boasting about His strength, Hanuman humbly expressed gratitude for the opportunity to serve. He attributed all His success to Rama's grace.

After the victory in Lanka, Rama embraced Hanuman and showered Him with praise. Rama declared that no one could repay Hanuman for His devotion and service. Hanuman, instead of accepting the praise for Himself, bowed down and said that serving Rama was His highest reward. He remained devoted without any desire for recognition.

Rama and Sita wished to offer Hanuman a precious gem-studded necklace as a token of Their gratitude. Hanuman, however, politely declined the offer. His only treasure was the opportunity to serve Rama and chant His name.

These acts show His detachment and humility, demonstrating that His devotion was not for reward but for pure love. True humility lies in working quietly and letting the action speak rather than the ego seeking praise.

Ego is often described as the false sense of self, the idea that we are separate from others and the world around us. It creates an illusion of superiority and control, causing us to constantly seek validation, recognition, and material rewards. In doing so, it builds walls between us and the Divine, between us and others, and ultimately, between us and our true selves.

We can acknowledge our strengths but not let them define us. We can focus on the greater good, contributing to society with the awareness that we are part of a much larger plan. When we succeed, we give credit where its due, whether to our mentors, parents, teachers, or the Divine.

We can practice humility by seeing the divine spark in everyone and everything around us. Instead of placing ourselves above others, we can embrace a sense of equality and understanding, respecting all people and living beings.

No ego, no recognition,
just pure devotion to a greater purpose.

I try to practice humility in my daily interactions, recognising that everyone has something to teach me. Even the smallest creatures, like an ant, demonstrate perseverance, teamwork, and resilience. By observing the world with an open heart, we can gather valuable lessons from every experience.

When Hanuman entered Lanka to find Sita, He could have immediately attacked Ravana. However, He waited, observed, and acted righteously. He first tried to convince Ravana with wisdom, showing that violence should be the last option. His righteousness ensured that He only engaged in battle when all peaceful options failed.

Hanuman's approach also reminds us of the importance of emotional restraint and patience. In moments of provocation, it's easy to respond impulsively. However, true strength lies in maintaining composure and responding with wisdom. By pausing to reflect rather than reacting in anger, we create space for better choices.

Practicing patience doesn't mean tolerating wrongdoing, but rather addressing challenges from a place of inner balance. Just as Hanuman's calm resolve led to the most effective course of action, we too can navigate difficulties with grace and purpose.

Willpower & Perseverance

Hanuman's unwavering willpower and legendary perseverance offer us a timeless lesson in the strength of determination and the triumph of the spirit. He teaches us the importance of persistence and the power of determination in achieving our goals. His undying resolve to help Lord Rama, regardless of the difficulty, demonstrates that nothing is impossible when one's intentions are pure.

The story of Hanuman leaping across the vast ocean to find Sita in Lanka is one of the most remarkable demonstrations of divine power. Hanuman's journey represents not just physical strength but also spiritual energy, willpower, intelligence, and unwavering devotion, all of which are aspects of inner strength.

Upon reaching the seashore, the Vanara army hesitated, doubting their ability to cross the vast ocean. At this moment, Jambavan, the wise elder, reminded Hanuman of His infinite potential, which He had forgotten due to a curse in His childhood. As Jambavan praised Hanuman's strength, wisdom, and divine abilities, Hanuman gradually awakened to His true power. The moment He realised His strength, Hanuman grew in size, radiated divine energy, and took a powerful leap across the ocean. This reminds us that divine power already exists within us, but we must awaken it through faith and self-awareness.

No obstacle could stop Him, whether it was Surasa, who tested His intelligence; Simhika, who tried to pull Him down with her shadow-capturing power; or the mighty waves of the ocean.

Surasa was a divine serpent and the mother of all serpents. Her encounter with Hanuman is another significant episode in the Ramayana, which took place during His leap across the ocean to Lanka in search of Sita. As Hanuman was flying over the ocean, the gods, wanting to test His strength, determination, and intelligence, sent Surasa to challenge Him. Surasa emerged from the ocean and took on a fearsome form, blocking Hanuman's path. She declared, "The gods have granted me a boon that no one shall pass without entering my mouth. Today, I shall devour You!"

Hanuman humbly folded His hands and replied, "I am on Lord Rama's mission to find Sita. Please allow me to fulfil my duty, and then I shall return to you." Surasa, however, insisted. Realising that she would not relent, Hanuman decided to use His wit. He began to grow in size, and Surasa widened her mouth to match Him. Hanuman then suddenly shrank to a tiny form, swiftly entering and exiting her mouth, fulfilling her condition without harm. Surasa, impressed by Hanuman's intelligence, blessed Him and allowed Him to proceed.

Surasa represents challenges that arise even when we are on a righteous path, reminding us that perseverance and resilience are essential in overcoming the tests life presents. Just as Hanuman used wisdom and adaptability to face Surasa, we too can navigate modern challenges with composure and clarity, emerging stronger in our resolve. Hanuman's response demonstrates the importance of remaining calm using intelligence rather than reacting with aggression. Despite His strength, Hanuman maintained humility and respect for Surasa, acknowledging her divine role.

Hanuman also teaches us the power of adaptability in being able to change size. In life, our success often depends on how we adjust to different circumstances. Every obstacle can be overcome when we approach it with clarity, humility and resilience.

In contrast, Simhika was a powerful monstrous sea demoness and lived in the depths of the ocean. She had the terrifying ability to capture her prey by seizing their shadows. As Hanuman soared above the ocean, Simhika noticed His massive form and immediately decided to devour Him. Using her mystical powers, she caught hold of Hanuman's shadow, rendering Him motionless. Though momentarily restrained, Hanuman remained calm. He quickly realised the nature of Simhika's power and understood that brute strength alone wouldn't suffice. With His sharp intellect and immense courage, Hanuman rapidly shrank His form to a tiny size and entered Simhika's mouth. Then, with explosive force, He expanded back to His gigantic size, tearing her apart from within.

This swift and strategic defeat of Simhika symbolises Hanuman's ability to overcome obstacles using not only His strength but also His wisdom and presence of mind. This story teaches us to conquer our inner demons.

Simhika represents negative forces like envy, ego, and jealousy that try to pull us down. Just as she held onto Hanuman's shadow, these negative tendencies latch onto our minds, preventing progress.

Hanuman had the power of awareness. His quick thinking and decisive action teach us the value of staying mindful and calm in challenging situations. By doing so, we can find the best solution with clarity and confidence. Despite her terrifying appearance, Hanuman faced Simhika without fear. His faith in Lord Rama gave Him the strength to triumph. This encounter is often meditated upon for strength, courage, and clarity in overcoming personal and external challenges. It's a reminder that with faith and inner strength, no obstacle is insurmountable.

When Ravana's army tried to capture Hanuman, they set His tail on fire. Instead of feeling defeated, Hanuman used this as an opportunity. He burned down Lanka, leaving a fiery warning that divine power cannot be defeated. His shakti was fuelled by unwavering faith in Lord Rama. Shakti is not just external force; it is inner courage, fearlessness, and divine protection. Hanuman shows that when we surrender to a higher power, we become limitless. His energy destroys negativity, removes obstacles, and protects us from harm.

Hanuman's leap across the ocean is a powerful reminder that power is already within us, but we must awaken it through faith, wisdom, and self-belief. Shakti must always be used for righteousness, never for ego or selfish gain. Unshakeable determination leads to success in any endeavour.

Challenges are opportunities to prove our strength and grow beyond our perceived limitations. I constantly remind myself of this point when faced with challenges. Set a goal and pursue it will full commitment. When facing obstacles, remind yourself: 'Hanuman never gave up!'

When we surrender to a higher power,
we unlock the limitless potential within,
transcending all boundaries.

Healer & Compassion

Hanuman is revered as a healer, capable of restoring health, vitality, and balance. His act of lifting the Dronagiri mountain symbolises the immense power of devotion and selflessness in the healing process. His healing abilities remind us that divine grace can cure not only the body but also the heart and soul.

When Hanuman could not identify the sanjeevani herb, He decided to carry the entire mountain back to Rama. In the context of healing, it teaches us that sometimes, instead of narrowly focusing on one solution, it is wiser to embrace a comprehensive approach. Just as Hanuman brought the whole mountain, ensuring no possibility of failure, holistic healing involves addressing the body, mind, emotions, and spirit together.

Today, practices like yoga, meditation, sound therapy, and herbal medicine embrace this holistic view, promoting overall well-being by harmonising all aspects of our being. True healing often requires the courage to explore multiple paths, incorporating natural remedies, emotional support, spiritual grounding, and medical care when necessary.

Similarly, healing in any form, be it physical, mental, or spiritual, requires faith in the process and the belief that the divine energy can flow through us to heal ourselves and others. For instance, countless people turn to prayer, meditation, or spiritual practices during health challenges, drawing strength and resilience from their faith. This connection to the Divine not only aids physical recovery but also brings emotional and spiritual peace. True healing is done selflessly, and it flows from a place of love and compassion.

Trust that His presence is a constant,
lifting us when we need it most.

My experiences with holistic healing have shaped my understanding of well-being. I reduced my dependency on modern medicine when I realised that some of my ailments were merely being treated symptomatically rather than holistically, which is why I wasn't seeing lasting results. This led me to explore Ayurveda, which proved to be much more beneficial for my health.

This realisation brought to mind Hanumanji's act of bringing the entire sanjeevani mountain because He was unsure which herb was needed to heal Lakshmana. In a profound sense, it reminded me that no single medicine holds all the answers. True healing involves addressing the root cause and working towards complete well-being.

Hanuman's unwavering concern for Lakshmana's recovery and His relentless efforts despite obstacles taught me the essence of genuine care. This reminds us that in modern healing, a strong sense of faith and dedication can foster resilience and inner strength, supporting recovery on both physical and emotional levels.

His act shows us that healing is not just about medicine; it's about love, care, and the divine energy that flows when we act with pure intent. I've often reflected on this when witnessing the lack of compassion in some hospitals and care centers, where patients may be treated mechanically without the love and warmth they truly need.

A particular experience stands out. I once visited a stroke patient who, after breakfast, had been left alone, gazing at the garden, the assumption being that he was enjoying the view. The nurse told me that they left him out in the sun every day, believing it made him happy. But when I looked at him, I felt sadness. He didn't seem happy, in fact to me he appeared helpless, maybe even hopeless.

I began to sing, and something unexpected happened. His vacant gaze shifted from the garden to me, tears welled up in his eyes, and I noticed his fingers beginning to move. He even attempted to sing along. That moment affirmed the immense power of love, presence, and compassion in healing. It was as though, in that instant, a divine force awakened within him.

In truth, I did nothing extraordinary. I simply responded to what I felt. But reflecting on it later, I realised that the power in that moment did not come from me, it flowed through me. Just as Hanumanji never claims credit for His heroic deeds but attributes everything to Rama, I too, felt like a mere instrument through which something greater was expressed. I didn't lift a mountain, but perhaps a burden was lifted from that soul. And that I believe, is the kind of spiritual strength Hanuman represents, strength that uplifts gently, rooted in devotion, not ego.

That quiet offering of song was not about performance or praise, it was simply an offering of the heart. And perhaps that is what gave it power. Hanumanji's example teaches us that true service asks for no recognition. It simply flows from love, fuelled by devotion and presence.

In hindsight, I understand that Hanumanji is always present, ever alert, ever aligned with the needs of the moment. When I saw that patient, I was guided not by my mind but by something more intuitive. That kind of presence allows divine grace to enter.

Such is the grace of Hanumanji, the divine servant whose strength lies not merely in might, but in the quiet, unwavering love that restores what is broken. In moments where despair hangs heavy, His spirit reminds us that healing can flow through the smallest acts of sincere presence. To be an instrument, even briefly, in restoring someone's spirit is to glimpse the sacred work Hanumanji performs eternally for Rama, for the world, and for every soul in need.

During my air travels, I find great comfort in chanting the mantra:

ॐ वायुपुत्राय नमः।

Om Vayuputraya Namah

Salutations to the son of the wind god Vayu.

Chanting this mantra before a flight invokes Hanumanji's protection for a safe and secure journey. Since He is the son of Vayu, the wind god, it brings calmness, courage, and reassurance during travel. Just as He offers strength and healing to those in need, He offers protection and comfort to those on the move.

Swami Tulsidas, the author of Ramcharitmanas, once suffered from intense pain in his arms. When no remedy worked, he turned to Hanuman and composed a hymn of forty-four verses known as Hanuman Bahuk in His praise. He recited each verse as he penned it, and remarkably with each recitation, he felt a gradual alleviation of his intense arm pain, which vanished entirely upon completing the verses.

Spiritual Teacher & Guide

Hanuman is also revered as a Guru, a divine teacher who guides seekers towards the path of spiritual wisdom and discipline. His knowledge and deep devotion to Lord Rama make Him an ideal spiritual guide. Hanuman teaches us the importance of discipline, dedication, and humility in our own spiritual journeys.

Hanuman represents the guru within, the inner guide that helps us overcome arrogance and ego. He teaches that knowledge without humility is incomplete. A guru, like Hanuman, does not just give answers but leads us to self-realisation through experience.

One instance of this is His interaction with Bhima, one of the Pandavas in the Mahabharata. While traveling through a forest, Bhima, known for his immense strength, came across an old monkey lying on the path, obstructing his way with his tail. Annoyed, he asked the monkey to move, but the monkey requested that Bhima move his tail instead. Bhima, proud of his strength, tried to lift the tail, but failed.

The monkey then revealed Himself as Hanuman, Bhima's elder brother, as both were sons of Vayu, the wind god. Hanuman humbled Bhima, teaching him that true power is not just physical strength but also wisdom, humility, and devotion, qualities essential for effective leadership and personal growth.

Hanuman's action was intentional but not ego-driven. He knew Bhima's nature to be fiery, that he was proud of his strength, and perhaps needing a gentle spiritual nudge. Hanuman purposefully appeared in the form of an old monkey on Bhima's path.

This lesson serves as a reminder that true strength often lies in understanding and respecting others, making thoughtful decisions, and leading with integrity. Before making important decisions, take a moment to sit in silence, close your eyes, and reflect on Hanuman's qualities. Visualise His presence and seek His guidance, allowing inner clarity to emerge from your contemplation.

Hanuman never procrastinated. When given a task, be it leaping to Lanka, finding Sita, or burning Lanka, He acted immediately, with full faith and energy. He teaches us the power of prompt action when dharma calls.

Procrastination often comes from doubt or laziness. Hanuman was always focused on His service to Shri Rama. When our purpose is clear and devotion is strong, procrastination dissolves. Hanuman symbolises speed, strength and timely action, qualities that destroy delay and indecision. Even the wind god, Vayu, cannot match His swiftness. That's why He's invoked by students and workers who want to overcome laziness and distractions.

At first glance, this point might seem out of place in this chapter but let me explain why it belongs.

Once, as I sat amidst delayed chores, and a list of unfinished tasks, a thought crossed my mind. I turned to Him: What would You do in my place? Answers do come!

*Turn to Him, He walks with you,
uplifts you, and never lets you fall.*

Hanuman, the mighty servant of Shri Rama, did not wait for the "right mood" or a more "convenient time." When Rama asked, "Will You go to Lanka?" Hanuman didn't say, "Maybe tomorrow, after some rest." He folded His palms and said, "At this moment, Prabhu!" In a single leap, He crossed the ocean not just of water, but the ocean of hesitation, laziness, and fear!

Procrastination delays the divine plan. Hanuman teaches us that time is sacred. If the Lord whispers a task into your heart today, do it today. Don't let self-doubt or fatigue rob you of spiritual growth. He is the one who flies across oceans not because He has wings, but because He has devotion, determination, and discipline.

So today, invoke Hanuman not just to remove ghosts and fears, but to remove clutter, laziness, and the excuses that hold us back. Chant His name, clean that corner of your room, finish that one task you've delayed and whisper in your heart: "Jai Hanuman Gyan Gun Sagar!"

5

The Power of Chanting & Sound Vibration

Sound has the power to heal, transform, and protect. Hanuman's name is not just a word, it is a force of strength, courage, and devotion. Whether chanted, written, or listened to, it acts as a spiritual shield, bringing clarity, peace, and divine energy into our lives. So, the next time you face doubt, fear, or stress, simply say: "Jai Hanuman!" Let His name be your meditation, mantra, and source of inner power.

In Vedic philosophy, naad or sound is considered the first form of creation. The universe itself has emerged from the cosmic sound 'Om'. Every name and mantra vibrates at a particular frequency, influencing both the internal aspects like mind and emotions, and the external such as energy and environment.

Modern studies in neuroscience show that chanting mantras or sacred names activates the parasympathetic nervous system, leading to reduced cortisol levels, the hormone associated with stress, while increasing focus, clarity, and a sense of peace and balance.

Chanting "Jai Hanuman" repeatedly and rhythmically synchronises brain waves, bringing a deep sense of calm. As Hanuman is the embodiment of fearlessness, His name also carries that energy. Hence, chanting His name invokes that same energy within us, boosting confidence and courage. His name creates a protective energy field, shielding us from negative influences.

The Hanuman Chalisa is one of the most recited prayers, known for its ability to bring protection, strength, and healing. But why is it so powerful?

Written by Swami Tulsidas with divine inspiration, its forty verses hold deep spiritual energy. It follows a rhythmic mathematical pattern, creating vibrations that affect the body and space around us.

What is the mathematical pattern? Chalisa literally means "forty." The main body of the text consists of forty chaupais or rhymed couplets. Each couplet has two lines. Each line has sixteen syllables, giving each couplet a total of thirty-two syllables. This follows the Chaupai Chand poetic meter in classical Hindi poetry. The Chalisa begins with two dohas or rhymed quatrains, each with two lines of twenty-four syllables, one doha at the start and one at the end.

Why this structure matters spiritually? The consistent sixteen syllable rhythm creates a resonant, musical vibration. Chanting rhythmically aligns breath, sound and intention, creating a vibrational field that is said to purify and energise the mind and space. Such rhythmic meter also activates specific chakras and induces a meditative state.

Even listening to the Hanuman Chalisa can purify the mind and surroundings, as the sound vibrations elevate the environment's energy. Chanting even one verse a day can make a difference if one does not have the time in schedule to complete the full Chalisa.

6

5-Day Hanuman Awakening Plan

In today's fast-paced world, we often become so engrossed in work, family responsibilities, and other commitments that we neglect the time needed to rejuvenate ourselves. Through my own experiences, I've learned that consistency is the key to achieving meaningful results. When we focus on something with dedication and repeat it consistently, we naturally attract its energy into our lives.

With this in mind, I have designed a suggested five-day program to help you discipline yourself in invoking Hanuman's energy. Feel free to adapt it to your schedule or create your own personalised plan. Practicing at a fixed time daily can be especially beneficial, as both the mind and body respond positively to a regular routine. Stay committed, and you'll soon notice the positive effects.

Day 1

Intention & Presence

With devotion in the heart and purity in thought,
even the mightiest obstacles are lifted.

Daily Intention:
Begin by setting a clear and heartfelt sankalpa, an intention to cultivate the divine qualities of Hanumanji within yourself: strength, humility, service, unwavering devotion, and fearlessness.

Reflection:
Read about Hanumanji's divine aspects in this book. Pause to reflect on His qualities, how they resonate with you, and how you might embody them in your daily life. Let this be a moment of inner inquiry and connection.

Practice:
Read, recite, or listen to the Hanuman Chalisa today.
Choose a version that touches your heart. Whether it's a classical rendition, a bhajan-style chant, or a modern musical interpretation, let it move you. As a singer, I often sing the Hanuman Chalisa, and I've noticed how new melodies flow through me spontaneously. I truly believe this is His way of reciprocating, inspiring my voice with His divine presence.

Sacred Listening:
While reading or listening, be fully present. Avoid multitasking. Do not treat this as background music. Instead, dedicate this time to immersing yourself in the prayer with complete awareness. When you give it your undivided attention, the spiritual energy is magnified and its meaning begins to blossom within your heart.

Chalisa Lyrics:
You will find the full text of the Hanuman Chalisa in the appendix at the end of this book, both in Devanagari and Roman scripts. If possible, try to learn the

Devanagari script. Each letter carries a subtle vibrational potency that is often lost in transliteration. While the Roman script is helpful, the depth and power of the original syllables are far more transformative.

Day 2

Breath & Inner Strength

The breath is the bridge between body and spirit,
a sacred current flowing through the temple of the soul.

Daily Intention:
Today, focus on harnessing your inner strength through the breath. Breath is prana, the life force which by cultivating awareness of it, you awaken your inner power. Even ten minutes of breath work can make a profound difference when done with consistency and reverence.

Cleansing & Centering:
If it suits your routine and health, begin your day with Jalneti kriya, a traditional yogic nasal cleansing practice. It clears the nasal passages, removes impurities, and prepares the body for deeper pranayama and meditation. If you have nasal sensitivities or medical concerns, consult a healthcare provider first. To perform Jalneti you will need a neti pot, distilled or previously boiled lukewarm water and non-iodised salt (1 tsp per 500ml).

Mix the salt in water until fully dissolved. Fill the neti pot. Lean over a sink, tilt your head sideways. Insert the spout of the neti pot into the upper nostril. Breathe through your mouth as the water flows from one nostril to the other. Repeat on the opposite side. Gently blow out excess water.

Pranayama – Anulom Vilom (Alternate Nostril Breathing):
Sit comfortably with a straight spine. Use your right hand to guide your breath. Close your right nostril with your thumb, with index and middle fingers resting on the forehead. Inhale through your left nostril. Close left nostril with ring finger and exhale through right nostril.

Now inhale through right, close it, exhale left. This is one round. Repeat for 5-10 minutes with calm, steady breaths.

Feel the transformation. Over time, you'll notice clearer breath, sharper mental focus, and deeper inner balance.

Sacred Practice:
After your breath work, return to the Hanuman Chalisa. Read it. Listen to it. Sing it. Let it envelop you in sacred sound.

Mantra Meditation:
You may also wish to chant or reflect on the following mantra:

ॐ श्री हनुमते नमः

Om Shree Hanumate Namah

Salutations to the auspicious Lord Hanuman.

Visualization:
As you chant, close your eyes and visualize a radiant golden light within your heart. See Hanumanji standing before you, powerful and serene. Let His energy enfold you in protection and courage.

Closing the Practice:
Offer a moment of gratitude to Hanumanji. Take a few gentle breaths, open your eyes slowly, and carry this divine strength into your day.

Day 3

Deepening the Connection

Devotion is not mere feeling; it is the strength to leap oceans, the wisdom to act with purpose, and the love to serve without pride.

Daily Intention:
Having anchored yourself in breath and intention, today you begin to deepen your connection with Hanumanji through the stories of His divine pastimes, most notably those described in the Sundara Kanda, the fifth book of the Ramayana.

The Beauty of Hanumanji:
The word Sundara means beautiful, and indeed, every aspect of Hanuman's actions in this Kanda reflects divine beauty. Here are a few radiant jewels from the Sundara Kanda to hold in your heart.

- Hanuman's Leap to Lanka: With undaunted courage, Hanuman crosses the vast ocean in search of Sita.

- Wisdom and Patience in Lanka: Surrounded by danger, He moves with alertness and restraint, revealing His inner wisdom.

- Consoling Sita: Upon finding Mother Sita in Ashoka Vatika, He becomes a bearer of hope, bringing Rama's message of love and assurance.

- Strength and Heroism: After His mission, He blazes through Lanka, fearlessly confronting evil.

- The Essence of Bhakti: Every action of Hanuman's in the Sundara Kanda radiates the purest form of selfless devotion.

Spiritual Reading and Listening:
Even if the stories are new to you, begin by listening to discourses from realised souls or reading commentaries on the Sundara Kanda. Absorb them with the heart, not just the mind. These tales are not mythology! They are living teachings meant to awaken divine attributes within you.

Meditation:
As you sit in silence today, meditate on these divine qualities:

- Devotion with discipline
- Faith and determination
- Strength tempered by humility
- Selfless service imbued with love

Reflection Practice:
Keep a notebook or journal beside you. As thoughts, emotions, or inner memories surface, gently write them down.

Reflect on:

- Where have I shown these qualities before?
- Where can I invite Hanumanji's example into my life now?
- What past moments need healing through strength and grace?

Allow Hanuman's shining example to guide your inner journey. His story is a mirror, showing you the infinite power and love that already exists within.

Day 4

Calling with Urgency

When the world feels heavy and your spirit feels faint, cry out with faith, for Hanuman answers the deepest call of the heart.

Begin as before:
Start your day with the pranayama from Day 2. Practicing Anulom Vilom regularly clears the nadis, the energy pathways, allowing your inner being to align with the divine current of strength and clarity. Let each breath become a preparation for prayer.

Invocation through Sound – Bajrang Baan:
After breath work, move into your sound practice for the day. Recite the Bajrang Baan aloud with conviction. Sing it, letting each note express your devotion or listen to a soulful rendition, absorbing the vibrations deeply. The Bajrang Baan is not a gentle hymn. It is a fierce and urgent call, a sacred arrow of sound aimed at the heart in distress. It is said when all other means feel weak, the Bajrang Baan pierces through darkness with the might of Hanuman's thunderbolt. It is often recited during moments of intense fear or turmoil, when one feels surrounded by negative energies or spiritual blockages, to seek immediate protection from unseen forces and to invoke courage and divine strength in a crisis. Bajrang means the one with a body like a thunderbolt and baan means arrow.

The Bajrang Baan was composed by Swami Tulsidas, who also wrote the Ramcharitmanas and the Hanuman Chalisa. Like much of his work, this hymn is in the Awadhi language, and you'll find the full lyrics in the appendix for regular use.

Post-Practice:
Sit in stillness for a few minutes. Let Hanumanji's protective energy settle within and around you.

Reflect:

- What am I facing today that feels too big for me?
- Where in my life do I need courage?
- What am I ready to hand over to Hanuman?

Let His shield of strength wrap around you, filling you with calm confidence and divine fire. Carry that energy into your day.

Day 5

From Prayer to Conversation

Speak to Him, and you will feel Him.
Trust in His nearness, and you will know His presence.

The journey of devotion is not only about rituals and recitations, but more importantly about relationship. By now, through your dedicated practice over the past four days, you may have felt flickers of peace, inspiration, or even resistance. These are signs that something within is awakening.

Today, you take a sacred step forward: begin a dialogue with Hanumanji.

"But how do I talk to Him?" This simple question carries profound power. It invites a shift, from looking outward to turning inward.

In the world outside, we use our eyes to see, our ears to hear, and our mouth to speak. But in the world within, the heart hears, the soul sees, and love speaks.

Begin today by reflecting on your practice so far:

- What arose for you during pranayama or chanting?
- Did you feel moments of peace, clarity, longing or even inner resistance?
- Were there quiet whispers of insight that came and went?

Take time to journal. Let the pen flow, don't edit, don't filter. Let it be raw, honest, and full of your essence.
Write whatever arises:

- "Today I feel…"

- “What I experienced during chanting was…”
- “I wonder why I felt uneasy when…”
- “Hanumanji, are You listening?”

If writing doesn’t resonate today, try something beautifully simple: Speak to Him. Out loud.

Yes, really speak aloud, as though He is right there before you. Because He is. Hanumanji is always listening with infinite patience, compassion, and presence.

Let your conversation be natural, like speaking to a trusted friend or a wise guide.
You might say:

- “Hanumanji, I’m unsure about what I felt yesterday…”
- “Thank You for helping me feel strong during that situation…”
- “Please give me clarity on…”
- “I’m afraid of what lies ahead…”

There is no right way, no perfect prayer. There is only sincerity. There is only you and Him. This practice matters. It builds intimacy with the Divine. It strengthens trust in the unseen. It nurtures the tender roots of devotion. It teaches you that you are never alone.

Acknowledge His presence. Even just softly saying, my

dear Hanumanji, I know You are here with me," can bring an energetic shift in your heart. The more you speak, the more you begin to hear, not in sound, but in feeling, in clarity, in the quiet assurance that He is with you.

Five days. One awakening.
You now sit with Him.
In silence, in strength, in surrender.
Jai Hanuman

7

Simple Worship and the Power of Manas Puja

Once we begin to establish a relationship with a deity, it's only natural to feel the desire to express our devotion through worship. However, when we're balancing work, family responsibilities, and other commitments, we may feel torn between our duties and our longing to perform puja or worship. The good news is that worship doesn't have to be complicated. Even the simplest act, when done with sincerity, reaches the Divine.

A traditional puja involves offerings like flowers, incense, water, and light. But what if you don't have access to these items? Manas puja, the act of offering everything within your mind, is a profound and equally powerful practice. Many great saints and sages have performed manas puja, demonstrating that devotion transcends material rituals.

Manas puja is not a lazy alternative, but a heartfelt offering in times when acquiring the necessary items is genuinely impossible.

Items needed for a simple worship are:

- A Hanuman deity or image, preferably one that clearly depicts His full form.

- Red flowers & sandalwood paste.

- A ghee lamp & incense.

- Jaggery or bananas as an offering.

Sit in a quiet place, light a lamp, and chant Om Shri Hanumate Namah. Offer flowers and incense, and gently apply a small amount of sandalwood paste to Hanuman's forehead or chest as a mark of reverence. Recite the Hanuman Chalisa, then close your eyes and visualize Hanuman's golden, radiant form. Seek His blessings to overcome fear, challenges, and negativity.

Remember, what matters most in puja is your bhava, your feeling and the purity of your heart and intention. Whether with elaborate offerings or through the simplicity of manas puja, the Lord accepts everything with unconditional love.

May Hanuman's unwavering devotion inspire you to cultivate a deeper, more intimate relationship with Him.

8

Alternative Meditative Practices

There are many ways to experience meditation, for example, through colouring, drawing, singing, writing, and movement. In this chapter, we explore how these creative and mindful activities can help connect with Hanuman's divine energy, deepen focus, and bring inner peace.

Colouring is a simple yet powerful meditation technique. As we colour, our minds naturally quiet down, allowing us to become absorbed in the present moment. This practice reduces stress, improves concentration, and encourages creativity and self-expression, all while deepening our devotion. Choose colours mindfully. Use red for strength and courage, yellow for wisdom and knowledge, and blue for peace and devotion. While filling in His image, visualize His qualities: loyalty, humility, and power. With each stroke, consciously imbibe those qualities within yourself. Reflect on the stories of Hanuman as you colour, deepening your connection with Him.

Drawing or sketching Hanuman, even in a simple form, can become a spiritual act of devotion. In ancient traditions, sacred art was used to focus the mind on God. Sketch with love. No artistic skill is necessary. Even simple outlines can be powerful when drawn with devotion. Chant while drawing. Repeating "Jai Hanuman" or "Shri Ram" while drawing can elevate the experience. Let go of perfection. The goal is devotion, not artistic excellence. This practice enhances concentration and transforms drawing into a sacred offering.

Music and sound are profound tools for achieving inner peace and devotion. Singing or even humming a Hanuman bhajan can create positive vibrations within the body and mind. Choose a Hanuman bhajan and sing with sincerity and love. Even if you prefer not to sing, listening to devotional music with closed eyes can be deeply meditative. Chant His name. Repeating "Jai Hanuman" softly can bring mental clarity and emotional balance. The sound vibrations uplift the soul and align your energy with divine frequencies.

Writing about Hanuman or reflecting on His qualities cultivates self-awareness and deepens devotion. When you write your thoughts and experiences, you may recall instances of Hanuman's presence in your life that previously went unnoticed. Journaling regularly enhances gratitude and strengthens spiritual growth.

Gentle movements inspired by Hanuman's qualities can become an active form of meditation. Even playing the Hanuman Chalisa in the background and physically enacting its lines can be deeply stimulating. Dance with devotion, even simple swaying movements, performed with love and joy, can enhance your connection. Yoga poses inspired by Hanuman, such as Hanumanasana, build focus and physical strength while invoking His divine energy.

Embracing these alternative meditative practices allows

you to experience Hanuman's presence in diverse and meaningful ways. Each act becomes a pathway to inner peace, devotion and spiritual growth.

9

Say Bye to Bullying ~ Hanuman Style!

Bullying is a challenge that many children face, whether through harsh words, exclusion, or physical harm. However, the life of Hanuman offers powerful lessons on how to respond to difficult situations with courage, wisdom, and resilience. By understanding Hanuman's qualities, children can learn to navigate bullying in a balanced and empowering way.

Hanuman was renowned for His incredible physical strength, but His true strength was His inner resilience. He used His might only when necessary, guided by His unwavering sense of justice. When bullied, children should remember their inner strength. Just like Hanuman did not tolerate wrongdoing, they too can stand up for themselves and others. Encourage children to practice assertiveness by using confident body language, maintaining eye contact, and speaking calmly. Teach them to say, "Stop. That's not okay" or "Please don't speak to me like that."

Hanuman was not only strong but also wise. He understood when to apply force and when to use diplomacy. Similarly, children can learn to assess situations carefully. Not every situation requires a physical or verbal response. Sometimes, walking away or seeking help is the wisest choice. Teach children to identify when they feel unsafe and to seek support from a trusted adult, such as a teacher, counsellor, or parent.

Despite facing immense challenges, Hanuman's unwavering determination allowed Him to succeed. Encourage children to cultivate self-confidence through positive affirmations like, "I am strong like Hanuman," and practice deep breathing or mindfulness exercises when feeling overwhelmed.

"I am strong like Hanuman"

Hanuman's deep devotion to Shri Rama gave Him purpose and courage. He knew who He served and why, and that gave Him the strength to face any challenge. In the same way, children can find inner strength when they feel supported by family, friends, or their faith. Facing bullying is not something they have to do alone. Let them know it's okay to speak up. Encourage open conversations about their feelings and experiences. Remind them that seeking help is not a weakness, it's an act of courage.

While Hanuman displayed immense power, He used it responsibly to protect others and stand against evil. Defending oneself is sometimes necessary, but it should always be done without anger or revenge. Teach children that physical self-defence is only justified when they are in immediate danger and cannot escape. Encourage them to enrol in self-defence classes for confidence and safety.

Emotional wounds from bullying are real and need care and healing. Encourage children to talk about their feelings, journal, or practice calming activities like listening to music, drawing, or spending time in nature.

Just as Hanuman sought counsel from Jambavan before His leap to Lanka, children should feel comfortable seeking help when they need it. Asking for support is a courageous step, not a weakness. Encourage them to identify three trusted people they can talk to when facing bullying.

To truly empower our children, we must begin early. Let

us not wait for challenges to arise before introducing them to the wisdom of our scriptures.

Stories like that of Hanuman are not just mythological tales, they are timeless guides to inner strength, resilience, compassion, and righteous action. When children grow up hearing about Hanuman's unwavering devotion, His courage guided by love, and His strength rooted in service, they naturally begin to embody these qualities.

Let's weave these teachings into their daily lives, so they don't just learn how to respond to adversity but they grow into individuals who carry the light of strength and wisdom into every stage of life.

10

Legends and Symbolism of Lord Hanuman

Unlocking layers of spiritual wisdom that transcend time and place, this chapter invites you to look beyond the familiar tales and discover the profound layers of meaning woven into every aspect of Hanuman's being.

From the mysterious origins of His name to the radiant symbolism of His red form, and the powerful significance of His five-faced manifestation, each facet unveils timeless spiritual truths that He teaches through silent example. In exploring these sacred nuances, we come to see why Hanuman is not merely worshipped, but deeply loved as the one who serves without pride, protects without hesitation, and dwells eternally in the heart of the Divine.

The Origin of Hanuman's Name

The name Hanuman has its roots in Sanskrit where 'hanu' means jaw, and 'maan' refers to something prominent or disfigured.

According to legend, as a child, Hanuman mistook the sun for a ripe fruit and tried to seize it. Lord Indra, attempting to stop Him, struck Hanuman with his thunderbolt, injuring His jaw. This incident gave Him the name Hanuman, meaning "one with a prominent or disfigured jaw."

Hanuman's original name was Anjaneya, meaning the son of Anjana. His mother, Anjana, was a celestial being cursed to be born as a vanara or monkey-like being on earth. After intense penance and prayers to Lord Shiva, she gave birth to Hanuman, hence the name Anjaneya, reflecting His maternal lineage.

The Sacred Reason Behind Hanuman's Orange Hue

One belief is that the colour symbolises strength and power, representing Hanuman's immense courage and energy. As one of the most powerful deities, His orange appearance is a visual reflection of His fiery nature and unwavering devotion.

Another explanation links Hanuman to the planet Mars (Mangal) in Vedic astrology. Mars, known for its aggressive and dynamic qualities, is associated with the colour red. Since Hanuman is considered to have a strong connection with Mars, His orange-red complexion is a symbolic representation of this cosmic relationship.

A popular legend further explains Hanuman's orange colour. One day, Hanuman noticed Mata Sita applying sindoor, or vermilion, to Her forehead. Curious, He asked Her about its significance. Sita explained that She applied sindoor to ensure the long life and well-being of Her husband, Lord Rama. Out of His profound love and devotion, Hanuman smeared His entire body with sindoor, believing it would grant Lord Rama an even longer life.

Why is Lord Hanuman Called Pawan Putra?

Hanuman is often referred to as Pawan Putra, meaning 'Son of the Wind', because He is the son of Vayu, the wind god.

When Anjana performed severe penance, Vayu was deeply impressed by her dedication. Upon Lord Shiva's command, Vayu played a divine role in the birth of Hanuman, blessing Him with immense strength, agility, and speed. Consequently, Hanuman is honoured as Pawan Putra, symbolising His celestial connection.

He is also known by other names such as Maruti, which relates to Vayu, the wind deity; Bajrangbali or Bajrangi, meaning one whose body is as strong as a thunderbolt; and Chiranjivi, the eternal one who lives forever.

Why is Lord Hanuman Not Married?

Lord Hanuman is revered as a brahmachari, a celibate devoted entirely to selfless service and unwavering devotion to Lord Rama. His life's purpose was to assist Rama in rescuing Sita from the demon king Ravana.

His celibacy symbolises supreme discipline, self-control, and spiritual focus.

Why is Lord Hanuman Called Balaji?

In regions like Rajasthan, Madhya Pradesh, and Haryana, Lord Hanuman is worshiped as Balaji, meaning 'child deity.' This name celebrates Hanuman's miraculous childhood deeds.

When Hanuman mistook the sun for a ripe fruit, Indra, the king of the gods, struck Hanuman with his thunderbolt, causing Him to fall unconscious. This enraged Vayu, Hanuman's father, who withdrew the air from the universe. Faced with impending disaster, the gods pleaded with Vayu for forgiveness. To pacify him, they restored Hanuman's life and bestowed Him with divine powers and immortality. Devotees worship Balaji Hanuman as a symbol of divine strength and protection.

One of the most renowned temples dedicated to Balaji is the Mehandipur Balaji Temple in Rajasthan. Hanuman resides here, offering protection from negative energies and evil spirits. According to tradition, Hanuman appointed Pretraj Sarkar as the ruler of spirits, and together, they assist devotees in overcoming malevolent forces.

The Significance of Hanuman's Mace, Tail, and Muscular Form

Hanuman's gada (mace) is a symbol of strength, authority, and divine power. It represents His ability to protect devotees and destroy evil forces. The gada is often seen as a reminder that righteous strength, when used with humility and devotion, can overcome even the most formidable challenges.

His tail, which played a significant role in the burning of Lanka, symbolises limitless power and resilience. Hanuman's tail was so long and powerful that Ravana's forces were unable to subdue it. It serves as a metaphor for the unbreakable spirit and determination required to overcome adversity.

Hanuman's muscular form represents not only physical strength but also inner fortitude. His well-built physique is a reflection of His disciplined life, unwavering faith, and devotion to Lord Rama. It conveys the belief that true strength comes from a heart filled with devotion and purpose.

Days Dedicated to Lord Hanuman

Tuesday is traditionally dedicated to Lord Hanuman. This day is associated with the planet Mars, which represents strength, courage, and determination, all qualities deeply embodied by Hanumanji. Mars is considered a fiery and aggressive planet, and those facing challenges like manglik dosha or Mars-related imbalances often turn to Hanumanji for relief and protection.

Though this story is not found in the Ramayana, it is well-loved in Puranic literature and regional folklore, making Saturday another deeply auspicious day for

Hanuman worship. According to a popular legend, Lord Hanuman once freed Shani Dev from the captivity of Ravana. During the war between Lord Rama and Ravana, Shani Dev was imprisoned out of Ravana's fear of his powerful planetary influence. When Hanuman set Lanka ablaze during His search for Sita, He came upon Shani Dev in captivity and liberated him. Grateful for this act of compassion, Shani Dev promised that Hanuman's devotees would be protected from the harsh effects of Shani Dosha, Saturn's challenging period, if they worshipped Him with true devotion.

In certain traditions, Wednesday is seen as a day to seek Hanuman's blessings for mental clarity, focus, and communication skills, as the planet Mercury governs intellect and expression.

In many spiritual lineages that emphasise devotion, wisdom, and discipline, Hanumanji is also worshipped on Thursdays, especially for His unwavering loyalty and the divine knowledge He carries.

My personal reflection is that while different days carry different energies, I believe that every day is a day of devotion. The heart doesn't follow a calendar. Chanting the Hanuman Chalisa daily is a powerful and protective practice, one that strengthens the mind, uplifts the spirit, and aligns us with divine grace, regardless of the day of the week.

Panchmukhi Hanuman: The Five-Faced Form

In the Ramayana, Lord Rama and his brother Lakshmana were taken to the netherworld, Patal Loka, by Ahiravana under the orders of Ravana. Hanuman, determined to protect them, ventured into Patal Loka to search for them but could not locate the brothers. After some investigation, Hanuman learned that the only way to rescue them was to defeat Ahiravana, whose life was hidden within five lamps placed at different corners of the room. To extinguish them simultaneously and end Ahiravana's life, Hanuman transformed into Panchamukhi Hanuman, assuming five faces: Hayagriva, Narasimha, Garuda, Varaha, and His own, Hanuman. This powerful form allowed Him to extinguish all the lamps at once and vanquish the demon, ultimately saving Lord Rama and Lakshmana.

Each face symbolises a divine aspect and has a unique significance:
Hanuman (Face of Courage and Strength): The central face represents unwavering devotion and fearlessness.
Narasimha (Face of Protection): Symbolises power and victory, this face wards off evil and protects devotees.
Garuda (Face of Detachment and Focus): This face provides protection from snake-related fears and obstacles.
Varaha (Face of Earthly Prosperity): Signifies wealth, health, and well-being.
Hayagriva (Face of Wisdom and Knowledge): The horse-headed face symbolises divine knowledge and wisdom.

Apart from Rameshwaram, you can also find other temples with Panchamukhi Hanuman in places like:

- Sri Panchamukha Anjaneya Temple in Kumbakonam, Tamil Nadu.
- Mantralayam, Andhra Pradesh (near the shrine of Raghavendra Swamy).
- Panchamukhi Anjaneya statue at Bidanagere, Kunigal, near Bangalore, Karnataka which is 161 ft tall.

South-facing Hanuman

Hanuman faced south when He defeated Ahiravan, a demon in the netherworld. Worshiping Him in this form is believed to protect devotees from negative energies. When Lord Hanuman traveled to Lanka in search of Sita, He faced the south. His confrontation with Ravana and the subsequent destruction of Lanka are symbolised through this southward gaze.

South-facing Hanuman is a fierce guardian, often invoked to dispel black magic and ward off evil spirits. The south is traditionally associated with Yama, the god of death, and is also believed to be the direction of negative energies. Hanuman's south-facing form symbolises His victory over death and darkness. He guards devotees from illnesses, accidents, and evil influences.

Famous south-facing Hanuman temples include:

- The Karmanghat Hanuman Temple, located in Hyderabad, Telangana. Built in the 12th century during the reign of the Kakatiya dynasty, this temple has since drawn countless devotees seeking protection from negative forces.

The story goes that King Pratap Rudra of the Kakatiya dynasty once ventured on a hunting expedition. After a long day, the exhausted king rested beneath a tree. While sitting in the stillness of the forest, he suddenly heard the divine chanting of Lord Rama's name. Curious and captivated, the king followed the sound deep into the jungle. To his astonishment, he discovered a stone deity of Lord Hanuman, who appeared to be meditating while chanting the name of Lord Rama. Overwhelmed by devotion, King Pratap Rudra bowed before the deity and returned home.

That night, the king had a vision of Lord Rama, who instructed him to construct a temple at the very spot where he had found the deity. Following this divine command, King Pratap Rudra laid the foundation for the temple the next day, establishing the Dhyana Anjaneya Swamy Temple in approximately 1143 AD. The deity of Lord Hanuman in deep meditation was enshrined at its heart.

Centuries later, during the reign of the Mughal Emperor Aurangzeb, the temple faced the threat of destruction. Determined to raze the structure, Aurangzeb's soldiers arrived in Hyderabad. However, despite their repeated efforts, they were mysteriously unable to even approach the temple. Every attempt was thwarted by an invisible force that pushed them back.

When the soldiers reported their failure to Aurangzeb, he grew furious and decided to demolish the temple himself. Armed with tools, he stormed the site. But, just like his men, Aurangzeb found himself unable to step inside. At that moment, a divine voice echoed through the air, proclaiming in Hindi: "Mandir todna hai to pehle, tum karo man ghat," meaning, "O King, if you wish to destroy this temple, first strengthen your mind."

Shaken and humbled, Aurangzeb dropped his weapons as a radiant light engulfed the temple. Witnessing this divine manifestation, he accepted his defeat. From that day onward, the temple became known as Karmanghat, a name derived from the words "Kar Man Ghat," meaning "Strengthen your Mind."

To this day, the Karmanghat Hanuman Temple stands as a testament to unwavering faith and divine protection, drawing pilgrims from across the country to experience its powerful presence.

- Shri Hanuman Jakhu Temple, Shimla (Himachal Pradesh). At 8,000 feet above sea level, this temple houses a massive statue of Hanuman, which faces south. Hanuman rested here while searching for the sanjeevani herb.

- Mehendipur Balaji Temple, Rajasthan. Known for rituals to cleanse individuals from negative energies and spirits, this south-facing Hanuman temple is visited by thousands seeking spiritual protection.

Why Hanuman Appeared on Arjuna's Chariot

The events described in Vedic literature do not all occur within the same cycle of creation. The universe passes through endless cycles of creation and dissolution, known as kalpas, and within each, many of the same divine pastimes reoccur, though the details and sequences may vary slightly.

According to the oral tradition passed down through the ages, there is a beautiful and profound story of a meeting between Hanuman and Arjuna, two great devotees of the Supreme Lord, appearing in different yugas, yet bound by divine purpose.

Before the great Kurukshetra war, Arjuna journeyed into the Himalayas to seek divine blessings. On this sacred path, he encountered Hanuman. As they spoke, Arjuna, curious and somewhat proud of his own archery skills, questioned Hanuman's unwavering devotion to Lord Rama.

"If Lord Rama was such an extraordinary archer," Arjuna asked, "why did He rely on the Vanaras to build a bridge to Lanka? Could He not have constructed it with His arrows?"

Hanuman replied with deep reverence, "Lord Rama is the supreme master of all skills. But He never acts out of pride. His actions are always in harmony with dharma. The building of the bridge was an opportunity to engage His devotees in His mission."

Still, Arjuna insisted, "I believe I could build a bridge

strong enough with my arrows."

Sensing the rise of ego in Arjuna, Hanuman decided to teach him a lesson in humility. He said, "Very well, let us see. Build a bridge across this small pond. If it holds my weight, I will agree with your claim. But if it doesn't?"

Arjuna boldly replied, "Then I shall sacrifice my life by self-immolation."

Arjuna constructed a bridge of arrows, confident in his abilities. But the moment Hanuman placed one foot on it, the entire bridge collapsed. True to his word, Arjuna, humiliated and heartbroken, prepared to end his life.

At that very moment, a wandering sanyasi appeared and asked what was happening. Hearing the story, he said, "You must not take your life. There were no witnesses. Rebuild the bridge, and let there be one now."

Hanuman agreed, and Arjuna rebuilt the bridge with careful devotion. This time, as Hanuman stepped onto it, the bridge remained firm. When He looked below, He saw a tortoise holding it up. In a flash, the sanyasi revealed Himself as Lord Krishna.

"I am Rama, and I am Krishna," the Lord said. "It was I who supported the bridge, just as I shall support both of you in the great war to come. Let this be a lesson in humility, Arjuna. Even the most skilled must remain free of pride. And Hanuman, though your devotion is true, compassion must temper even correction."

Both Hanuman and Arjuna fell at Krishna's feet in

gratitude and repentance.

"As a sign of unity and protection," Krishna continued, "Hanuman, you shall ride on the banner of Arjuna's chariot during the Mahabharata war."

And so it was. Throughout the war, Hanuman stood atop Arjuna's chariot—silent, strong, and ever watchful—symbolising unwavering devotion, strength, and divine grace.

Is Hanuman Still On Earth?

Yes, Hanuman is still present on this Earth. Hanumanji is considered a Chiranjivi, one of the eight immortals who are said to remain on earth until the end of this Kali Yuga, for the protection of dharma and the support of true devotees.

Chiranjivi literally means 'long-living' or 'immortal'. These beings are believed to remain in their physical or subtle forms, unseen to most, but present and active.

In the Ramayana, Lord Rama Himself blesses Hanuman:"Wherever my story is told, Hanuman, you will be present there listening, blessing, and uplifting."

Over the centuries, many saints, sages, and yogis including Tulsidas, Ramdas, and even modern-day seekers have shared stories of receiving Hanumanji's darshan or guidance during deep meditation, crisis, or spiritual practice.

Hanumanji may not be seen by all, but His presence is felt by those who approach Him with faith and sincerity. Whether in subtle form, vision, or inner strength, He reveals himself when the heart is pure.

11

From Valmiki to Tulsidas

Tulsidas and Valmiki are two revered saints and poets in Indian tradition, both known for their monumental contributions to the Ramayana's literary and devotional landscape.

While the exact date of Valmiki's birth is unknown, it's believed he lived around 500 BC. He is regarded as the Adi Kavi, the first poet, of Sanskrit literature. He authored the Valmiki Ramayana, the original epic that narrates the life story of Lord Rama in Sanskrit. The epic consists of 24,000 verses divided into seven books, or kandas.

He composed the first-ever verse in Sanskrit out of spontaneous sorrow when he witnessed a hunter killing a bird: "Ma Nishada!" (O hunter, may you never find peace!)
This emotional outburst marked the birth of his poetic expression and also the beginning of Sanskrit verse literature.

Valmiki is also a personality in his own Ramayana. It was in his hermitage that Sita sought refuge after her exile, and he raised her twin sons, Lava and Kusha. He educated the boys, and they later sang the Ramayana in Lord Rama's court without initially revealing their identity.

Before becoming a sage, Valmiki was known as Ratnakara, a ruthless highway robber. He attacked travellers to support his family. One day, he tried to rob the divine sage Narada. Instead of cursing him, Narada asked him a profound question: "Will your family share the burden of your sins?" When Ratnakara realised that no one would, he was deeply shaken.

Narada advised him to meditate and chant the name of Lord Rama. According to legend, due to his inner impurities, he was unable to say Rama and instead began chanting Mara, which means death. Gradually, this transformed into Rama.

Valmiki's life demonstrates that even the most sinful individuals can attain enlightenment through repentance
and devotion. His story is often cited as an example of how divine grace can transform a person.

Tulsidas was born in the 16th century in Rajapur (modern-day Uttar Pradesh). Upon birth, instead of crying, he uttered the name of Rama, earning him the name Rambola.

Tragically, his father passed away on the fourth night after his birth, and his mother abandoned him. A maid named Chuniya took him to her village, Haripur, and raised him until her death five and a half years later.

Left an orphan, Rambola survived by begging for alms.

His spiritual journey was guided by Narhari das, who renamed him Tulsidas. He later studied Sanskrit grammar, literature, and philosophy under Shesha Sanatana in Varanasi.

According to legend, he was the reincarnation of Valmiki, as mentioned in the Bhavishyottar Purana. Hanuman, devoted to listening to Valmiki's Ramayana, eventually guided Tulsidas to Lord Rama.

It was during a discourse that Tulsidas recognised Hanuman, who then directed him to Chitrakuta, where he had a divine vision of Rama and Lakshmana. One morning, as Tulsidas was making sandalwood paste, Rama approached him for a tilak, a sacred mark on the forehead, marking a profound spiritual encounter. Inspired by divine visions, Tulsidas wrote the Ramcharitmanas in Awadhi rather than Sanskrit, making the epic accessible to the common people. He began writing it in Ayodhya on Ram Navami in 1631 and completed it in 1633. The work was later presented at the Kashi Vishwanath Temple, where Lord Shiva and Parvati blessed it.

Tulsidas passed away at Assi Ghat in Varanasi in 1623.

Appendix

The Hanuman Chalisa and Bajrang Baan are both powerful devotional hymns dedicated to Lord Hanuman, but they differ in purpose, tone, structure, and energy.

Hanuman Chalisa tone is sweet, gentle, and reverent. It praises Hanuman as a devotee par excellence and seeks His grace for spiritual upliftment.

Bajrang Baan is full of mantric power to tear through darkness and fear. It praises Hanuman as the fierce protector and the destroyer of evil. The devotee invokes Hanuman's warrior form with urgency and intensity.

श्री हनुमान चालीसा

॥ दोहा ॥

श्रीगुरु चरण सरोज रज, निज मनु मुकुरु सुधारि ।
बरनऊँ रघुबर बिमल जसु, जो दायकु फल चारि ॥
बुद्धिहीन तनु जानिके, सुमिरौं पवनकुमार ।
बल बुद्धि बिद्या देहु मोहिं, हरहु कलेस बिकार ॥

॥ चौपाई ॥

जय हनुमान ज्ञान गुण सागर । जय कपीस तिहुँ लोक उजागर ॥
राम दूत अतुलित बल धामा । अंजनिपुत्र पवनसुत नामा ॥
महाबीर बिक्रम बजरंगी । कुमति निवार सुमति के संगी ॥
कंचन बरन बिराज सुबेसा । कानन कुंडल कुंचित केसा ॥
हाथ बज्र औ ध्वजा बिराजै । काँधे मूँज जनेऊ साजै ॥
शंकर सुवन केसरीनंदन । तेज प्रताप महा जग बंदन ॥
विद्यावान गुनी अति चातुर । राम काज करिबे को आतुर ॥
प्रभु चरित्र सुनिबे को रसिया । राम लखन सीता मन बसिया ॥
सूक्ष्म रूप धरि सियहिं दिखावा । बिकट रूप धरि लंक जरावा ॥
भीम रूप धरि असुर सँहारे । रामचंद्र के काज सँवारे ॥
लाय सजीवन लखन जियाये । श्रीरघुबीर हरषि उर लाये ॥
रघुपति कीन्ही बहुत बड़ाई । तुम मम प्रिय भरतहि सम भाई ॥
सहस बदन तुम्हरो जस गावैं । अस कहि श्रीपति कंठ लगावैं ॥
सनकादिक ब्रह्मादि मुनीसा । नारद सारद सहित अहीसा ॥
जम कुबेर दिगपाल जहाँ ते । कबि कोबिद कहि सके कहाँ ते ॥
तुम उपकार सुग्रीवहिं कीन्हा । राम मिलाय राज पद दीन्हा ॥
तुम्हरो मंत्र बिभीषन माना । लंकेस्वर भए सब जग जाना ॥
जुग सहस्र जोजन पर भानू । लील्यो ताहि मधुर फल जानू ॥

प्रभु मुद्रिका मेलि मुख माहीं । जलधि लाँघि गये अचरज नाहीं ॥
दुर्गम काज जगत के जेते । सुगम अनुग्रह तुम्हरे तेते ॥
राम दुआरे तुम रखवारे । होत न आज्ञा बिनु पैसारे ॥
सब सुख लहै तुम्हारी सरना । तुम रक्षक काहू को डरना ॥
आपन तेज संहारो आपै । तीनों लोक हाँक तें काँपै ॥
भूत पिसाच निकट नहिं आवै । महाबीर जब नाम सुनावै ॥
नासै रोग हरै सब पीरा । जपत निरंतर हनुमत बीरा ॥
संकट तें हनुमान छुड़ावै । मन क्रम बचन ध्यान जो लावै ॥
सब पर राम तपस्वी राजा । तिन के काज सकल तुम साजा ॥
और मनोरथ जो कोई लावै । सोई अमित जीवन फल पावै ॥
चारों जुग परताप तुम्हारा । है परसिद्ध जगत उजियारा ॥
साधु संत के तुम रखवारे । असुर निकंदन राम दुलारे ॥
अष्ट सिद्धि नौ निधि के दाता । अस बर दीन जानकी माता ॥
राम रसायन तुम्हरे पासा । सदा रहो रघुपति के दासा ॥
तुम्हरे भजन राम को पावै । जनम जनम के दुख बिसरावै ॥
अंत काल रघुबर पुर जाई । जहाँ जन्म हरिभक्त कहाई ॥
और देवता चित्त न धरई । हनुमत सेई सर्ब सुख करई ॥
संकट कटै मिटै सब पीरा ॥ जो सुमिरै हनुमत बलबीरा ॥
जै जै जै हनुमान गोसाईं । कृपा करहु गुरु देव की नाईं ॥
जो शत बार पाठ कर कोई । छूटहि बंदि महा सुख होई ॥
जो यह पढ़ै हनुमान चालीसा । होय सिद्धि साखी गौरीसा ॥
तुलसीदास सदा हरि चेरा । कीजै नाथ हृदय मँह डेरा ॥

॥ दोहा ॥

पवनतनय संकट हरन, मंगल मूरति रुप ।
राम लखन सीता सहित, हृदय बसहु सुर भूप ॥

Shri Hanuman Chalisa

Doha:
Shri Guru Charan Saroj Raj
Nij Man Mukuru Sudhari
Barnau Raghubar Bimal Jasu
Jo Dayaku Phal Chari

By cleansing the mirror of my mind with the dust of my Guru's lotus feet, I sing the pure glory of Lord Rama, which bestows the four fruits of life—dharma, artha, kama, and moksha and yet inspires one to transcend even liberation through divine love, bhakti.

Buddhiheen Tanu Jaanike
Sumirau Pavan Kumar
Bal Buddhi Vidya Dehu Mohi
Harahu Kalesh Vikar

Knowing myself to be ignorant, I remember Hanuman, the son of the wind god. Grant me strength, wisdom, and knowledge, and remove all my afflictions and impurities.

Chaupai:
Jai Hanuman Gyan Gun Sagar
Jai Kapis Tihun Lok Ujagar
Ram Doot Atulit Bal Dhama
Anjani Putra Pavan Sut Nama

Victory to Hanuman, the ocean of wisdom and virtue. Victory to the Lord of the monkeys, who illumines the three worlds. You are Lord Rama's emissary, an abode of incomparable strength, the son of Anjani and the wind god, Pavan.

Mahabir Bikram Bajrangi
Kumati Nivaar Sumati Ke Sangi
Kanchan Baran Biraj Subesa
Kanan Kundal Kunchit Kesa

O mighty, valiant one with a body like a thunderbolt. You remove evil thoughts and are a companion to those with pure minds. Your golden complexion glows with divine beauty with earrings in Your ears and curly hair.

Hath Bajra Aur Dhvaja Birajai
Kaandhe Moonj Janeu Sajai
Shankar Suvan Kesari Nandan
Tej Pratap Maha Jag Vandan

You hold a thunderbolt and a flag in Your hands, and wear a sacred thread across Your shoulder. You are the incarnation of Shiva and the son of Kesari. Your brilliance and strength are revered across the universe.

Vidyavan Guni Ati Chatur
Ram Kaj Karibe Ko Atur
Prabhu Charitra Sunibe Ko Rasiya
Ram Lakhan Sita Man Basiya

You are supremely intelligent, virtuous, and wise, always eager to serve Lord Rama. You delight in listening to Lord Rama's glories, You reside in the hearts of Lord Rama, Lakshmana, and Sita.

Sookshma Roop Dhari Siyahin Dikhava
Bikat Roop Dhari Lank Jarava
Bheem Roop Dhari Asur Sanhare
Ramchandra Ke Kaj Sanvare

You appeared before Sita in a small form, and assumed a fierce form to burn Lanka. You took a massive form to slay demons, and carried out Lord Rama's divine mission.

Laye Sajeevan Lakhan Jiyaye
Shri Raghubeer Harashi Ura Laye
Raghupati Keenhi Bahut Badai
Tum Mam Priya Bharat Hi Sam Bhai

You brought the sanjeevani herb and revived Lakshmana

delighting Lord Rama, who embraced You. Lord Rama greatly praised You, and said You are as dear to him as his brother Bharata.

Sahas Badan Tumharo Jas Gaavein
As Kahi Shripati Kanth Lagavein
Sanakadik Brahmadi Munisa
Narad Sarad Sahit Ahisa

Even a thousand mouths would fail to describe Your glory, Saying this, Lord Rama embraced You. The sages like Sanaka, Brahma, and other divine beings, Narada, Saraswati, and Shesha sing Your praise.

Jam Kuber Digpal Jahaan Te
Kavi Kovid Kahi Sake Kahan Te
Tum Upkar Sugreevahi Keenha
Ram Milaye Rajpad Deenha

Yama, Kubera, and the guardians of all directions, even poets and scholars are unable to describe Your glory. You did a great favour for Sugreeva, by introducing him to Lord Rama and helping him regain his kingdom.

Tumharo Mantra Bibhishan Maana
Lankeshwar Bhaye Sab Jag Jaana
Jug Sahastra Jojan Par Bhanu
Leelyo Taahi Madhur Phal Jaanu

Vibhishana accepted Your advice, and became the king of Lanka. As the world knows You leaped across a distance of thousands of yojanas to reach the sun, thinking it was a sweet fruit.

Prabhu Mudrika Meli Mukha Maahi
Jaladhi Langhi Gaye Acharaj Naahi
Durgam Kaaj Jagat Ke Jete
Sugam Anugrah Tumhare Tete

With Lord Rama's ring in Your mouth, You crossed the ocean

—a marvellous feat indeed. All difficult tasks in the world become easy by Your grace.

Ram Duaare Tum Rakhvaare
Hot Na Aagya Bin Paisaare
Sab Sukh Lahai Tumhari Sarna
Tum Rakshak Kaahu Ko Dar Na

You guard the gates of Lord Rama, No one can enter without Your permission. All happiness is attained by taking refuge in You. With You as protector, one has no fear.

Aapan Tej Samharo Aapai
Teenon Lok Haank Te Kaapai
Bhoot Pishach Nikat Nahin Aavai
Mahabir Jab Naam Sunavai

You alone control Your own immense power. At Your roar, all the three worlds tremble. Ghosts and evil spirits cannot come near, when the name of the mighty Hanuman is chanted.

Nasai Rog Harai Sab Peera
Japat Nirantar Hanumat Beera
Sankat Te Hanuman Chhudavai,
Man Kram Bachan Dhyan Jo Lavei

Diseases are destroyed and all suffering is removed, by continuous remembrance of Hanuman. Hanuman frees those from distress, who meditate on him with mind, action, and words.

Sab Par Ram Tapasvee Raaja
Tinke Kaaj Sakal Tum Saaja
Aur Manorath Jo Koi Lave
Soi Amit Jeevan Phal Pave

Lord Rama is the supreme king of ascetics, and You accomplish all His divine tasks. Whoever comes to You with desires, receives abundant blessings and fulfilment in life.

Charo Yug Partap Tumhara
Hai Parasiddh Jagat Ujiyaara
Sadhu Sant Ke Tum Rakhwaare
Asur Nikandan Ram Dulaare

Your glory is renowned in all four ages, and Your brilliance illuminates the entire world. You are the protector of sages and saints, the vanquisher of demons, and Lord Rama's beloved devotee.

Ashta Siddhi Nav Nidhi Ke Daata
Asa Bar Deen Janki Maata
Ram Rasayan Tumhare Paasa
Sadaa Raho Raghupati Ke Daasa

You are the bestower of eight divine powers and nine treasures, as blessed by Mother Sita. You hold the divine essence of Lord Rama within You and remain eternally devoted to Him.

Tumhare Bhajan Ram Ko Paave
Janam Janam Ke Dukh Bisraave
Anth Kaal Raghupati Pur Jaai
Jahan Janma Hari Bhakta Kahai

By chanting Your name, one attains Lord Rama's grace and is freed from the sufferings of many lifetimes.
At the end of life, one who remembers You will enter Lord Rama's divine abode and be reborn as his devotee.

Aur Devata Chitt Na Dharai
Hanumat Sei Sarva Sukh Karai
Sankat Kate Mite Sab Peera
Jo Sumire Hanumat Balbeera

No other deity needs to be worshiped by those who adore You, for You alone grant all happiness. All troubles vanish, and sorrows end for those who remember the mighty Hanuman.

Jai Jai Jai Hanuman Gosaai
Kripa Karahu Gurudev Ki Naai
Jo Shat Baar Paath Kar Koi
Chhoot Hi Bandhi Maha Sukh Hoi

Victory to You, O Lord Hanuman! Please bless us with Your grace as a revered teacher would. Whoever recites this Chalisa one hundred times with devotion will be freed from all bondage and attain immense joy.

Jo Yah Padhe Hanuman Chalisa
Hoye Siddhi Saakhi Gaurisa
Tulsidas Sada Hari Chera
Keejai Nath Hriday Mah Dera

Whoever reads this Hanuman Chalisa with faith shall attain divine fulfilment, with Lord Shiva as the witness. Tulsidas, the eternal servant of Lord Rama, prays for the Lord to reside in his heart.

Doha:

Pavan Tanay Sankat Haran
Mangal Moorati Roop
Ram Lakhan Sita Sahit
Hriday Basahu Sur Bhoop

O son of the wind god, remover of sorrows, embodiment of auspiciousness, May You reside in my heart, along with Lord Rama, Lakshmana, and Sita.

श्री बजरंग बाण

॥ दोहा ॥

निश्चय प्रेम प्रतीति ते, बिनय करैं सनमान।

तेहि के कारज सकल शुभ, सिद्ध करैं हनुमान

॥ चौपाई ॥

जय हनुमंत संत हितकारी। सुन लीजै प्रभु अरज हमारी॥

जन के काज बिलंब न कीजै। आतुर दौरि महा सुख दीजै॥

जैसे कूदि सिंधु महिपारा। सुरसा बदन पैठि बिस्तारा॥

आगे जाय लंकिनी रोका। मारेहु लात गई सुरलोका॥

जाय बिभीषन को सुख दीन्हा। सीता निरखि परमपद लीन्हा॥

बाग उजारि सिंधु महँ बोरा। अति आतुर जमकातर तोरा॥

अक्षय कुमार मारि संहारा। लूम लपेटि लंक को जारा॥

लाह समान लंक जरि गई। जय जय जय धुनि सुरपुर नभ भई॥

अब बिलंब केहि कारन स्वामी। कृपा करहु उर अंतरयामी॥

जय जय लखन प्रान के दाता। आतुर होइ दुख करहु निपाता॥

जय गिरिधर जय जय सुख सागर। सुर-समूह-समरथ भटनागर॥

ॐ हनु हनु हनुमंत हठीले। बैरिहि मारु बज्र की कीले॥

गदा बज्र लै बैरिहिं मारो। महाराज प्रभु दास उबारो॥

ॐकार हुंकार महाप्रभु धावो। बज्र गदा हनु विलम्ब न लावो॥

ॐ ह्रीं ह्रीं ह्रीं हनुमंत कपीसा। ॐ हुं हुं हुं हनु अरि उर सीसा॥

सत्य होउ हरि शपथ पायके। रामदूत धरु मारु धाय के॥

जय जय जय हनुमंत अगाधा। दुख पावत जन केहि अपराधा॥

पूजा जप तप नेम अचारा। नहिं जानत कछु दास तुम्हारा॥

बन उपबन मग गिरि गृह माहीं। तुम्हरे बल हम डरपत नाहीं॥
पाय परौं कर जोरि मनावों। यह अवसर अब केहि गोहरावों॥

जय अंजनि कुमार बलवन्ता। शंकर सुवन धीर हनुमन्ता॥
बदन कराल काल कुल घालक। राम सहाय सदा प्रतिपालक॥

भूत प्रेत पिशाच निशाचर। अग्नि बैताल काल मारीमर॥
इन्हें मारु तोहि शपथ राम की। राखु नाथ मरजाद नाम की॥

जनकसुता हरि दास कहावो। ताकी शपथ विलम्ब न लावो॥
जय जय जय धुनि होत अकाशा। सुमिरत होय दुसह दुःख नाशा॥

चरण शरण करि जोरि मनावों। यहि अवसर अब केहि गोहरावों॥
उठु उठु चलु तोहिं राम दुहाई। पांय परौं कर जोरि मनाई॥

ॐ चं चं चं चपल चलन्ता। ॐ हनु हनु हनु हनु हनुमन्ता॥
ॐ हं हं हांक देत कपि चञ्चल। ॐ सं सं सहम पराने खल दल॥

अपने जन को तुरत उबारो। सुमिरत होय आनन्द हमारो॥
यहि बजरंग बाण जेहि मारै। ताहि कहो फिर कौन उबारै॥

पाठ करै बजरंग बाण की। हनुमत रक्षा करै प्राण की॥
यह बजरंग बाण जो जापै। तासों ते भूत प्रेत सब कांपे॥

धूप देय अरु जपै हमेशा। ताके तन नहिं रहे कलेशा॥

॥ दोहा ॥

प्रेम प्रतीतिहिं कपि भजै, सदा धरै उर ध्यान।
तेहि के कारज सकल शुभ, सिद्ध करै हनुमान॥

Shri Bajrang Baan

Doha
Nishchay Prem Pratiti Te
Vinay Karei Sanmaan
Tehi Ke Kaaraj Sakal Shubh
Siddh Karei Hanuman

Those devotees who recite these verses with love and unwavering faith have all their beneficial desires fulfilled by Hanuman.

Chaupai
Jay Hanumant Sant Hitkaari
Sun Lije Prabhu Araj Hamari
Jan Ke Kaaj Vilamb Na Kije
Aatur Dauri Maha Sukh Dije

Glory to Hanuman, the benefactor of saints. Please listen to our prayer. Do not delay in doing the work of Your devotees. Please rush to do it and give us immense peace.

Jaise Kudi Sindhu Mahipaara
Surasa Badan Paithi Vistaara
Aage Jaay Lankini Roka
Maarehu Laat Gai Suraloka

Come running just like when You leapt across the ocean, entered and then emerged from the expanded mouth of Surasa [who tried to obstruct Your path], and on landing in Lanka sent the demoness Lankini to the heavenly abode by kicking her to death [when she tried to prevent You from entering the city].

Jaay Vibhishan Ko Sukh Dinha
Sita Nirakhi Parampad Linha
Baag Ujaari Sindhu Mah Bora
Ati Aatur Jamkaatar Tora

In Lanka You gave pleasure to Vibhishan [by meeting him] and attained the supreme position [of being loved by Sri Ram] due to Sita's merciful benediction. Then You destroyed the Ashoka grove and dumped the trees in the ocean, symbolically breaking the knife of Yama, the God of Death.

Akshay Kumaar Ko Maari Sanhaara
Loom Lapet Lank Ko Jaara
Laah Samaan Lank Jari Gai
Jay Jay Jay Dhuni Surpur Me Bhai

You killed Akshay Kumar (Ravana's son) and burnt Lanka with Your tail. Lanka burned like lac (molten wax) and the heavens were filled by the sound of "Hail to Hanuman's glory".

Ab Vilamb Kehi Kaaran Svami
Kripa Karahu Ur Antaryaami
Jay Jay Lakhan Pran Ke Data
Aatur Hoy Dukh Karahu Nipaata

Why are You delaying now my Lord; You know what resides in the minds of Your devotees, so have mercy on me. Glory to You who restored the life of Lakshman. Quickly dispel my fears.

Jai Giridhar Jai Jai Sukh Saagar
Sur Samuh Samarath Bhatnaagar
Om Hanu Hanu Hanumant Hathile
Bairihi Maaru Bajra Ki Kile

Hail to You, holder of the mountain! You are an ocean of happiness, wisest amongst gods and the most skilful. O You of indomitable spirit kill the enemies (lust, anger, greed) as if they were nailed by the strike of a thunderbolt.

Gada Bajra Lai Bairihi Maaro
Maharaj Prabhu Daas Ubaaro
Omkar Hunkaar Mahaprabhu Dhaavo
Bajra Gada Hanu Vilamb Na Laavo

O Lord! Relieve Your servant by hitting the enemies with Your mace as if it were a thunderbolt. Saying the thundering sound of OM, challenge the enemies and crush them with Your mace.

Om Hrim Hrim Hrim Hanumant Kapisa
Om Hum Hum Hum Hanu Ari Ur Shisha
Saty Hohu Hari Shapath Paayke
Ram Doot Dharu Maaru Jaay Ke

O Hanuman, Lord of the Monkeys, I invoke You with the Tantric mantra Oṁ hrīn hrīn hrīn and Oṁ hū̃ hū̃ hū̃. Strike the enemy in the chest and head. I swear by the name of Hari that all that I say is the truth. O messenger of Sri Ram, rush to attack the enemy at once.

Jay Jay Jay Hanumant Agaadha
Dukh Paavat Jan Kehi Aparaadha
Pooja Jap Tap Nem Achaara
Nahi Jaanat Hau Das Tumhaara

Glory to You, O fathomless Hanuman! Due to which offence is Your devotee suffering so much? This servant of Yours knows nothing of worship, sacred mantras, penance, or the discipline of rituals and virtuous acts

Van Upavan Mag Giri Grih Maahi
Tumhare Bal Ham Darapat Naahi
Paay Parau Kar Jori Manaavau
Yehi Avasar Ab Kehi Goharaavau

Relying on Your strength, I have no fear anywhere – whether in the forest, garden, mountains, on the road, or in the house. I fall at Your feet and entreat You with folded hands to help me. For whom else shall I call at this hour?

Jay Anjani Kumar Balvanta
Shankar Suvan Vir Hanumanta
Badan Karaal Kaal Kul Ghaalak
Ram Sahay Sada Pratipaalak

Hail Hanuman! All-powerful son of Anjani and brave son of Shiva. You have a fierce and terrifying body and are the slayer of even the God of Death's minions. You are always by the side of Sri Ram and are the benefactor of all.

Bhoot, Pret, Pishaach Nishaachar
Agni Betaal Kaal Maari Mar
Inhe Maaru, Tohi Shapath Ram Ki
Rakhau Nath Marjaad Naam Ki

Slay all evil spirits: ghosts, spirits, hobgoblins, demons, fire, vampires, calamities, and epidemics. Kill all of them in the name of Lord Sri Ram thereby maintaining the sanctity and truth of the holy name.

Janaksuta Hari Das Kahaavo
Taaki Shapath Vilamb Na Laavo
Jai Jai Jai Dhuni Hot Akaasa
Sumirat Hot Dusah Dukh Naasha

You are the servant of Sri Ram and Mother Sita. I implore You in their names – make no delay. The sky is reverberating with the sound of Your glories, the mere remembrance of which dispels all sorrows.

Charan Sharan Kar Jori Manaavau
Yahi Avasar Ab Kehi Goharaavau
Uthu Uthu Chalu Tohi Ram Duhaai
Pay Parau Kar Jori Manaai

I have come to take refuge at Your feet. I plead with You; who else shall I call for help in this time of urgent need? Get up, get up, come along! I urge You with folded hands to swing into action.

Om Cham Cham Cham Chapal Chalanta
Om Hanu Hanu Hanu Hanu Hanumanta
Om Han Han Haank Det Kapi Chanchal
Om San San Sahami Paraane Khal Dal

I implore You O nimble-footed Hanuman with the call of Oṁ chãṁ chãṁ chãṁ chãṁ and Oṁ hanu hanu hanu hanu. Strike swiftly like lightning! O Hanuman, You are swift. Whenever the monkeys roar, the crowd of evil-doers flee in terror.

Apane Jan Ko Turat Ubaaro
Sumirat Hoy Anand Hamaro
Yah Bajrang Baan Jehi Marei
Taahi Kaho Phir Kaun Ubaarei

Save this devotee of Yours immediately. I get immense pleasure remembering You. Who can save one who is attacked with the arrow of Bajarang Baan.

Path Karei Bajarang Baan Ki
Hanumat Raksha Karei Praan Ki
Yah Bajrang Baan Jo Japei
Taate Bhoot-Pret Sab Kaape

Those who recite these verses of Bajarang Baan are protected for life by Hanuman. Even ghosts and evil spirits tremble out of fear of those who chant this Bajarang Baan.

Dhoop Dey Aru Japei Hamesha
Taake Tan Nahi Rahe Kalesha

Those who wave incense sticks in front of You and chant Your holy name are always free from bodily torments of all kinds.

Doha

Prem Pratitihi Kapi Bhajei
Sada Dharei Ur Dhyaan
Tehi Ke Kaaraj Sakal Shubh
Siddh Karei Hanuman

Those who chant Hanuman's holy name with faith, devotion, and love and always remember him in their hearts are sure to have all their desires fulfilled by Hanuman.

Satsang is not just a gathering,
it's a return to our divine essence.

About the Author

Shashika Mooruth is an internationally acclaimed South African vocalist, composer, and spiritual seeker.

From a very young age, she was drawn to using her voice as a medium to spread peace, love, and harmony. Her first performance came at the age of eight, and by fourteen, she was already singing before thousands, raising funds for old age homes, orphanages, charitable trusts, and spiritual organisations across South Africa.

She later pursued a B.Sc part-time through the University of South Africa (UNISA), while immersing herself in Hindustani classical vocal and sitar training in India.

In 2003, she launched her independent label, URJA MUSIC, determined to bring forth her own original works. Since then, she has produced over 200 original songs and performed in more than 25 countries.

In 2018, she was honoured with the International Achiever Award by the President of South Africa,

Honourable Cyril Ramaphosa, at the 24th South African Music Awards (SAMA24), organised by the Recording Industry of South Africa. She became the first South African Indian to be recognised with this top honour for pioneering original works in traditional Indian music on the global stage.

But behind the glamour of awards and international acclaim lies a far deeper journey—one of devotion, spiritual discipline, and inner transformation. For nearly three decades, Shashika has lived in India, choosing a life steeped in the sacred. She often performs in temples, singing for hours in deep spiritual immersion.

Even while embracing the roles of mother, daughter, wife, and artist, Shashika remains unwavering in her spiritual discipline. She lives the understanding that sadhana is not confined to the Himalayas, rather it is a way of life. Though she has spent years in sacred spaces, she brings the essence of those experiences into every moment, transforming any environment into a spiritual sanctuary.

Her voice, shaped by years of inner and outer discipline, is more than music, it is vibration that uplifts the soul. She does not merely perform; she invokes. Each melody becomes a portal to stillness, joy, and divine presence. Whether singing classical, devotional, or contemporary pieces, her music resonates with higher consciousness.

Her life reflects a profound truth: the inner journey is what truly matters. Whether on global stages or in quiet contemplation, Shashika walks her path with grace.

In a world where fame often overshadows faith, Shashika Mooruth offers something rare: balance. She has not renounced the world, but rather, integrated it.

Through her music and her way of living, she inspires others to seek the Divine within, proving that the Himalayas can rise wherever the heart is ready to ascend.

To connect with Shashika Mooruth
visit her official website:

www.shashikamooruth.com

Scan the QR code below for direct access.

www.ingramcontent.com/pod-product-compliance
Ingram Content Group UK Ltd.
Pitfield, Milton Keynes, MK11 3LW, UK
UKHW021400190726
13845UKWH00028B/785